Radical Matter

Reconfiguration of a Tree
by Studio Thomas Vailly.

Radical Matter

Rethinking materials
for a sustainable future

**KATE FRANKLIN
AND CAROLINE TILL**

with over 280 illustrations

Thames & Hudson

Contents

Carole Collet

Design is dead.

Long live design.

For too many and for too long, design has been first and foremost associated with a styling exercise led by creative tensions between aesthetic and function. Consumerist propagation and exaggerated material cultures have quickly ostracized the teachings of designer-ecologists. I remember to this day my first encounter with Victor Papanek's proposition to design for the real world, embracing sustainable imperatives and addressing social and ecological interconnected needs. I had finally found a manifesto that resonated with my personal belief: that design and ecology should be an integrated practice. But somehow, towards the end of the 20th century, mainstream design ignored this holistic vision to the benefit of short-term consumerism and for the profit of global shareholders.

Nearly 20 years into this century, we can now proudly announce that a whole new chapter of design history is being rewritten. With sustainability and social welfare at its core, design has the power to change the world as we know it, and a new breed of designers are reinventing their practices and developing new ones to make a difference. Radical Matter captures this movement with brilliance. Enticing, provocative and at times 'mind-boggling', this book unravels ecological stories that can inspire and inform innovative ways of making and seeing. The following pages showcase radical approaches, creative collisions, extraordinary visions, tangent practices and everything from the exploitation of extreme waste (shit and dust), to working with living factories and reinventing future mining.

Above all, this book celebrates the abundance and generosity of creativity and breaks away from the notion that sustainable design is worthy and dutiful. If this book does not entice you to radically engage with sustainability, then I don't know what will.

Carole Collet

Professor of design for sustainable futures
and director of the Design and Living Systems
Lab Central Saint Martins, London

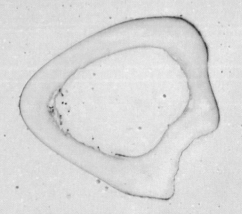

Introduction

Kate Franklin
and Caroline Till

Rethinking
Materials

Cumbrian Bone Marble by
Yesenia Thibault-Picazo.

We are potentially on the brink of a materials revolution that could help rebalance our relationship with our planet and reshape society for the better. Up to now, we have relied on a supply of natural raw materials that we transport to large factories and turn into products. We then ship those products around the world, where we enjoy them all too briefly and discard them when we no longer require them. This model is reaching its physical limits. We are running out of raw materials and creating enormous quantities of waste. We cannot continue to race through our planet's finite resources; indeed, all the evidence suggests that if we continue at our current rate, we'll soon need a second planet.

We need a better, smarter, more cyclical approach, in contrast to our current linear 'take–make–discard' relationship with materials – and a new future seems to be within our reach. Placing emphasis on materiality enables us to reconsider the building blocks of the design process from the bottom up. Thanks to a raft of exciting designers and makers who are fostering disruptive approaches, we are beginning to see that alternative systems of production and consumption are possible – and we are recognizing that material innovation will be crucial to achieving this.

In the quest for improved sustainability and enhanced performance, makers become alchemists, designers become scientists, and artisans become social entrepreneurs. All are crossing boundaries in the pursuit of a multidisciplinary approach; a spirit of collaboration is encouraging the exchange and sharing of knowledge and ideas.

While technological innovation is important, it is not the whole story. The advances of the future are rooted in the achievements of the past. The projects presented here embrace a full spectrum of materiality, from craft processes that would be recognizable to makers from previous centuries to cutting-edge smart and interactive tech. While there is everything to gain from looking forwards and planning for a better future, there is also much to learn from looking backwards – and, indeed, from looking sideways and re-evaluating what we already have.

The projects we present are eclectic but something they share in common is a hands-on approach where designers and makers explore major social issues by taking these concerns into their own hands. This proactive, can-do attitude encourages us to regain mastery over technology and places emphasis on process as well as on output. We are certainly not suggesting that this forum offers a global panacea, or anything approaching it: but we believe that small movements generate momentum and inspiration for wider action. Radical thinking on any scale can lead to great change.

Within this book we celebrate the designer and the maker as agents of change. While they acknowledge the previous contributions of their discipline to unsustainable systems, they are moving forward and seeking to tackle the issues of the 21st century head on. We are all becoming aware that the system needs a complete overhaul rather than tinkering at the edges. These designers and makers are using their skills to that end. Framed by a series of key ideas that pave the way towards a more sustainable material future, these projects champion radically different approaches.

1

Today's Waste, Tomorrow's Raw Material

—

Over-consumption of scarce resources is driving designers to reclaim materials from waste. As well as offering environmental benefits, these innovations signal a shift in our relationship with materials, away from a linear take–make–discard model to a more cyclical approach where designers harvest alternative raw goods from industrial and domestic waste streams and landfill.

Traditional raw materials are finite and expensive while waste is abundant and cheap, so it is perhaps no surprise that designers, brands and makers are turning their attentions to our household rubbish and industry's scrap as sources of innovative raw materials. Through predominantly mechanical processes, paper, concrete, leather, textiles and plastic are being redirected into cyclical systems that celebrate and capitalize on their inherent qualities.

Turning vice into virtue, plastic – that most pervasive and polluting material of modern life – is becoming one of the most recyclable. Brands and makers are exploiting its innate durability, malleability and indestructibility to create sound, hardwearing materials for a variety of purposes – the petroleum age's equivalent of fashioning silk purses from sows' ears.

In the home, consumers are being encouraged by the developers of new systems and machinery to regenerate their own household trash, creating cyclical home ecosystems that reduce the burden of domestic waste. Encouraging self-sufficiency, these initiatives are leading us towards a future when, according to artist and designer Daan Roosegaarde, 'waste should simply not exist…waste is a resource'.

Potentially recyclable materials are in abundant supply. In established fashion manufacturing, waste is rampant. Less than half of leather production is considered good enough for use as primary material; the remainder is discarded. Similarly, when making denim clothing, 15% of fabric is squandered during the cutting process.

And it's not just traditional industries that need to overhaul their processes. Our addiction to new technology, abetted by short product lifecycles and a culture of rapid upgrades, is creating a vast waste stream of discarded metals, glass, plastics and rare earth minerals. In America alone, some 9.4 million tons of electronic waste is trashed each year, leaving a huge potential resource untapped. According to the United States Environmental Protection Agency, from every million discarded cellphones an astonishing abundance of highly valuable metals – 16,000 kg (35,274 lbs) of copper, 350 kg (772 lbs) of silver, 34 kg (75 lbs) of gold and 15 kg (33 lbs) of palladium – could be recovered.

In the European Union, the latest figures reveal that the average citizen generates around half a ton of waste every year. Although recycling and composting efforts are reducing amounts sent to landfill, the overall quantity of discarded detritus is still rising. Most people recycle less than half their rubbish. In some European countries, households recycle almost nothing.

The statistics might be shocking, but they provide inventive designers and makers with unparalleled opportunities for exploiting the sheer abundance of discarded materials. By using intelligent, sensitive, appealing design, these waste pioneers are developing exciting and innovative ways to turn what has previously been unwanted into a variety of objects of desire.

However, unlike previous iterations of recycling and repurposing, this is no make-do-and-mend culture. The aesthetics achieved by these experimental interventions are the antithesis of typical upcycling and recycling. In most cases the waste matter is broken down and reconstituted to create an entirely different material resource that is highly refined and far removed from its origin.

In the fields of textiles and fashion, food production, furniture and construction, <u>Post-Industry Waste</u> is being reclaimed on both large and small scales. Here, designers are reworking waste to create new pieces and base materials, the provenance of which is often barely visible. More widely, brands and creative environmental agencies are waking up to the potential of rubbish. And it isn't just an industrial movement. Domestic adoption of open-source attitudes is aiding the development of <u>The Home Ecosystem</u>. Abetted by designers and developers of open-source machinery, environmentally conscious consumers are pioneering domestic recycling systems that refashion their domestic waste into new objects.

1

2

3

6

4

5

8

7

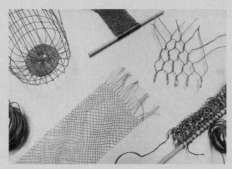

9

10

Post-Industry Waste

**Designers are reworking the by-products
of textile and fashion manufacturing, food
production, furniture and construction into new
pieces and base materials, the provenance of
which is often barely visible. Exploiting anything
from fibres and wood fragments to substantial
offcuts and industrial debris, this is material
reclamation across the spectrum of scale.
Size doesn't matter; as long as it exists in
sufficient quantity, the waste can be mined
as a new resource.**

1 — Material Illusions by Sophie Rowley
2 — Well Proven Chair by Marjan van Aubel and James Shaw
3 — Structural Skin by Jorge Penadés
4 — WasteBasedBricks by StoneCycling
5 — Materia Madura by Ana Cristina Quiñones
6 — Hot Wire Extensions by Studio Ilio
7 — NewspaperWood by Mieke Meijer

The Home Ecosystem

**Via open-source attitudes and tech, the home
is becoming a waste recycling ecosystem.
Environmentally conscious designers are
developing machinery that enables consumers
to remake their own domestic waste into
new objects.**

8 — Micro Urban Mining by Jorien Wiltenburg
9 — Precious Plastic by Dave Hakkens
10 — Joining Bottles by Micaella Pedros

Anders Lendager

Architect Anders Lendager
is the founder of Lendager
Group, an innovative company
that works in the built
environment, specializing
in cost-neutral sustainable
buildings with a special
focus on circular economy.

With so many more people squeezing on to the planet – 9.7 billion by 2050, according to the UN – attention is being focused on the lack of materials, water, food and energy. The question of how we can use these global problems as design engines is really important. In the period in which we designed the modern city, we used materials and energy without really thinking about them, or how we would cope without enough to create a new future. Finding solutions, when we have a structure that is based on this past ideology, is very difficult. That's the challenge we face today.

Without simple, immediate solutions, the call for action towards a systemic change is growing. If we see the challenge in terms of maker problems, then we need to ensure we find maker solutions. Ecologists and environmentalists always say to use less. We, however, envisage a whole integrated approach, encompassing innovation, growth and creating a sustainable economy, so that we can find solutions that don't change the way that we live and can be integrated in our current lifestyles. We need to look at materials differently, but without losing our capacity for innovation. If our lifestyle is threatened, the change becomes too radical to find workable solutions.

It follows that if we want to create change, we have to do it with strong **GDP** growth. It's one of the bedrocks of capitalism and the tool for change to happen faster. Fortunately, for the first time we are seeing countries increase their **GDP** at the same time as lowering CO_2 emissions, according to McKinsey. That's a new image for growth.

If this systemic change should happen – and it needs to happen – then we want people to use more stuff, but with a new way of looking at things. When the wrong materials and resources are pushed out of the equation by better, more sustainable materials and processes, we can build more sustainable buildings and cities. Then growth will start to happen.

An important way of looking at these new materials is to look at all the materials that we have already broken or brought into our cities. We have all the materials we need, they are already here. And true innovation can create new materials out of what we have and upcycle them to new values. Then we will start to see immense CO_2 reductions.

Today's waste can be made as desirable as the virgin materials of the past. For architects and designers, the chance of creating something beautiful from something that looks ugly and was designed badly is much greater than if they take something like a piece of 400-year-old oak and try to add beauty to it. We have done it with upcycled concrete. The used concrete makes the new concrete more beautiful. We sand it down and you see the old concrete as a lighter colour within the new concrete, like the rings in a tree. It becomes a kind of terrazzo concrete that is very beautiful, also because the narrative that it is reused is embedded in the material for everyone to see.

What we are looking for in sustainability is always this added value. It doesn't have to mean more investment. It has to be a layered story about why this material is more valuable. If we can do that, then we succeed in making a difference.

This page and opposite:

Designer Sophie Rowley
transformed hyper-common
waste matter, such as paper,
glass, textiles and foam,
into brand-new materials.
Through replicating the
process found in nature,
Rowley was able to simulate
the aesthetics of the natural
world, making the waste
desirable once again.

Material Illusions

Sophie Rowley

Sophie Rowley, a material designer and consultant, plays with the perception of materials. Regarding waste streams as 'a future quarry, a starting point rather than an end point,' Rowley mines 'non-virgin materials which already have had a life'.

Drawing on the aesthetics of natural processes, such as the layering of rocks and their transformation through erosion, Rowley re-engineers 'hyper-common' waste materials, such as denim, paper, styrofoam or glass to produce singular designs in which random patterns simulate the aesthetic of natural materials such as wood or stone, elevating the original resource until it is no longer recognizable.

Experimentation with materials and techniques led to unexpected but successful outcomes. 'The most surprising material for me was the blue foam,' says Rowley. 'I had managed to get it to a bubbly, plasticky blue piece of material. I then put it in the sandblaster and sanded it. When I took it out it looked so natural, like a blue coral. I was very surprised by that unexpected transformation.'

When she discarded all her failed material experiments, Rowley discovered she was left with samples that 'all fitted together very harmoniously. They all looked like very natural materials, such as stones, corals, shells. I continued to achieve these nature-like aesthetics with other materials. Often it was about replicating processes that we can see in nature, such as the layering of materials which you can see in the Earth's sediments.'

To create a bespoke interior stool, Rowley draped Diesel denim offcuts over a mould and bonded the layers with bio resin. After drying, she carved through the layers to create a flat surface in which the differing sizes and shades of the denim generated an intriguing marble-like pattern that gave the stool its name, the Bahia Denim, after a Brazilian blue marble that it resembles. In 2014, Rowley was commissioned by Nissan to fashion the Bahia Denim in the shape of a dashboard for an exhibition on sustainable materials of the future.

For another project, Rowley sourced glass production offcuts from a manufacturer in London. Broken down and fused in a kiln, the reclaimed ingredients merged into a material with individual textures and shades that Rowley describes as resembling the surface of the Argentinian Perito Moreno glacier. Her Perito Moreno Platters 'allow for an exciting colour palette and are great ornaments for the interior'.

Rowley's Silverwood Door Weight turns mundane local newspaper waste into an object with the aesthetic of timber. By adding material in layers, creating a tubular form, Rowley replicates the formation of tree-rings by 'leaving some areas trunk-like and carving others, which displays the surface contrast.' The result is striking and convincing. 'Paper, commonly perceived as a lightweight material, becomes the weight of a space,' says Rowley. 'Due to its blue-greyish colours it is named after the silverwood tree.'

sophierowley.com

TODAY'S WASTE, TOMORROW'S RAW MATERIAL

Below:

The Silverwood Door Weight is
named after the Californian
silverwood tree because
it is similar in colour and
pattern. The door weight is
made out of compressed layers
of commercial newspaper waste
in a cylindrical form.

Opposite, above:

The Bahia Denim pattern
is produced using waste
from Diesel's denim
production. The offcuts
are combined using a bio
resin and compressed to
create a solid material,
which can then be carved
and sanded to reveal
a grain-like pattern.

Rowley's Bahia Denim is
intended to resemble Bahia
Brazilian blue marble and
can be moulded into practical
and durable furniture pieces.

Opposite, below:

The Perito Moreno Platters
are composed of reclaimed
glass material sourced from
a local glass manufacturer in
London. The waste fragments
are broken down and fused
together in a kiln to create
a whole new blended material.
The platters, named after
their surface texture, bear
resemblance to the Perito
Moreno glaciers in Argentina.

The Well Proven Chair is
formed of waste wood shavings
and bio resin. When the two
combine, a natural chemical
reaction occurs causing
the mixture to foam before
solidifying.

Well Proven Chair

Marjan van Aubel and James Shaw

In 2012, Marjan van Aubel and James Shaw stumbled upon a surprising and bizarre foaming reaction that occurred between soya bio resin and sawdust waste harvested from their London workshop. The reaction caused the porridge-like mixture to expand significantly before setting into a strong, mouldable, lightweight foamed material.

Inspired by the realization that up to three-quarters of timber used in the furniture and wood-processing industries is discarded in the form of sawdust and wood chips, Van Aubel and Shaw set about looking for ways to make use of their serendipitous discovery. Further experiments revealed that using different types of wood chip and sawdust, adding water, trapping air in shavings, and increasing the temperature of the reaction caused expansion of up to seven times in volume.

The duo began experimenting with the colours of wood, investigating how best to show the material's natural beauty. The result is a series of stools that combine natural white ash, cherry and walnut timber legs, with hard foam seats made from sawdust and chips discarded in the making of the legs in their workshop. In a pleasingly cyclical manner, the same tonally matched timbers accentuate the colour and texture of the original and new materials.

Van Aubel and Shaw slapped the resin and shavings mixture onto the underside of the chair shell by hand, building up the material wherever extra strength was required. The mixture then foamed explosively to create its own exuberant form. They explain that they 'wanted to allow the material to express its natural beauty, rising up free form, contrasting with the controlled simplicity of the legs. The smooth surface of the seat contrasts with the geological wildness of the backs and undersides that expresses the material's exuberance in its foaming reaction.' The stools are available in three heights that are suitable for a dining table, worktable or bar.

wellprovenchair.com

Left:

Designer Jorge Penadés shreds scraps of leather from the fashion industry in a paper shredder before combining them with natural bone glue.

Below:

The glue-soaked strips are then pressed into a mould and left to set. The resulting robust planks are shaved to reveal strata of colourful blended material and bolted together to form structural furniture frames.

Structural Skin
Jorge Penadés

Jorge Penadés, who lives and works in Madrid, recycles leftovers and offcuts from the leather industry, which discards more than half of the animal hides it uses because they are considered to be not good enough to use as a primary material.

Drawn to leather 'because it's the first material in history that humans used,' Penadés said he was 'shocked' by the lack of well-established recycling processes. 'Leather is a beautiful material, but very inefficient in terms of its manufacturing process due to its natural origins. No matter which tanning process a hide went through, the quality of a piece of leather depends directly on the part of the animal that it came from. The higher the movement, the lower the quality.'

Exploiting the strength and beauty of apparently worthless leftovers, Penadés binds scraps of leather with natural bone glue to create a robust material that he has used to make furniture. Leather offcuts sourced from Hermès, after the French fashion house's pattern cutters have sliced their shapes, are fed through an office paper shredder. The thin leather strips are pressed into a long iron mould, soaked with bone glue, compressed and left to set. When removed from the mould, the resultant strut, shaved to reveal and emphasize the leather's material language and visual qualities, has the appearance (if not the texture or smell) of marble.

'To finish the material,' says Penadés, 'I used shellac, a natural resin that comes from an insect. After this, it's like wood and I can cut it and sand it. The fibres of the leather give it a slightly flexible quality, but it's pretty stiff.'

The glue binder is fully biodegradable, making the finished material entirely recyclable. The struts can be reprocessed and remoulded. Nothing is lost; everything is reusable. Penadés's Structural Skin project has led to several pieces, including a clothes hanger, a side table and an ornamental mirror, but he says it could also be used to create tiles, flooring and even shoe soles with a quite unexpected pattern.

jorgepenades.com

WasteBasedBricks

StoneCycling

Tom van Soest, co-founder of Dutch circular economy start-up StoneCycling, has all the attributes of an artisan chef. He spends his time concocting new recipes from unusual ingredients, which he bakes in an oven to produce a range of products that carry names familiar to any student of cuisine – Aubergine, BlueBerry, Salt, Lentil, Radish, Nougat and Salami.

But, as StoneCycling's name – as well as its product, WasteBasedBricks – suggests, the result of each recipe isn't at all digestible. Motivated by wanting to address the fact that construction accounts for a third of all waste in the European Union, van Soest recycles demolition waste to produce bricks. Combining rejected clay from traditional brick manufacturing with waste from the glass, ceramic and insulation industries, he has created a range of around 20 bricks in colours as exotic as their names.

Exact recipes used to make each type of WasteBasedBricks are secret, but the ingredients, all sourced from within 100 miles of his laboratory in the southern Netherlands province of Limburg, determine the finished brick's colour and aesthetics. Aubergine, a dark purple brick, carries white flecks. Radish's mottled red-brown appearance is very similar to the standard redbrick. Nougat, 70% of which is made of waste, comes in sliced and raw flavours depending on the size and number of the red-brown chips that fleck its cream-coloured base.

Recipes that work in van Soest's laboratory are tested to ensure compliance with market and regulatory technical demands, and are then scaled up for production in a nearby factory. Initially, StoneCycling's bricks found their way into table surfaces and a restaurant in Amsterdam, in which fragments of old Heineken bottles were crushed and mixed with other construction waste materials to produce a highly polished bar counter. In 2015, van Soest garnered his greatest vote of confidence when a Dutch architect couple commissioned him to produce the bricks for their home that they planned to build in the city centre of Rotterdam.

About 15,000 kg (33,000 lbs) of waste was upcycled to produce the Caramel Raw and Sliced variants of the WasteBasedBrick and in August 2016 the building, a three-storey terraced home that echoed the existing architecture of the street, was completed. Three months later, van Soest received the ultimate acclaim for his invention when, during Dutch Design Week, he won Young Designer at the Dutch Design Awards. The international jury said that 'what makes Tom van Soest's work so admirable is that he presents a usable product that offers true impact. In doing so, he stands out through his keenness to look beyond the end product and design the production process, too.'

Their citation continued: 'Van Soest is all the more praiseworthy for getting a grip on frequently time-consuming and complicated legislative processes for new construction materials, in a short space of time.'

stonecycling.com

Dutch company StoneCycling
has created WasteBasedBricks.
The bricks are produced
using locally sourced waste
construction material,
including rejected
clay, glass, ceramic and
insulation material. This
waste matter is blended,
reformed and baked into new
building supplies.

Ana Cristina Quiñones combines plantain and coffee grounds collected from restaurants and cafés in London to produce new material that is durable, functional, sustainable and biodegradable.

Materia Madura
Ana Cristina Quiñones

Many sparks of inspiration first strike in restaurants or cafés, but surely Materia Madura by Ana Cristina Quiñones must be one of the few clever ideas that can trace its source to the waste bins of those establishments. Studying and working as a material, product and furniture designer in London, Quiñones remembered the mountains of plantain peels and coffee grounds in her native Puerto Rico and decided she wanted to develop a model for tackling food and agricultural waste that would be globally transferable.

As staple foodstuffs in her homeland, plantain peels and coffee grounds are abundant and ubiquitous; living in London, Quiñones turned to a Cuban restaurant and some local cafés to source her raw materials.

Inspired by the indigenous Taíno culture of Puerto Rico and their prehistoric artefacts, Quiñones developed a collection of furniture and ornaments reminiscent of the Taíno people's musical instruments. 'I was interested in 16th-century European musical instruments and inspired by the unusual materials used like elephant ear skin, tortoiseshell, bone and carved pumpkins,' she says.

Using the material she had created from plantain and coffee waste, Quiñones says she 'started with a güiro, a traditional percussion instrument held in your hand and played with a stick. I redesigned it, changed the shape and made it ergonomic. The whole process further inspired the furniture.'

Quiñones constructed initial full-scale models of her designs in recycled clay, from which she made soft silicone shells and hard shells of Jesmonite, a gypsum-based material in an acrylic resin that is water-based, non-toxic and solvent-free. The malleable material derived from plantain peels and coffee grounds was then struck in the moulds. Materia Madura has proved to be durable and functional, sustainable, biodegradable and more lightweight than other materials of similar aesthetic qualities.

anacristinaquinones.com

Hot Wire Extensions
Studio Ilio

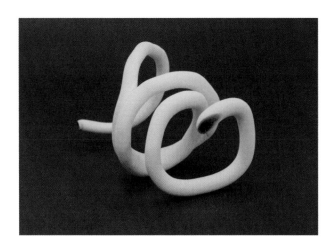

Fabio Hendry and Seongil Choi, graduates of the Royal College of Art in London, make chairs out of wire and powder – not just any old powder, but a combination of sand and waste nylon from the most popular form of 3D printing, Selective Laser Sintering (SLS). Now established as Studio Ilio, their design and manufacturing techniques offer the tantalizing promise that, by anticipating the waste streams of new production technologies and processes, we might one day design out waste before it comes into existence.

The duo met at the Royal College of Art where, assigned the first-year task of making a chair, they examined the process before the product. This prompted them to develop a new method of making furniture by exploiting a previously untried material.

They began their search in the college's bins, mining for discarded waste that might melt around electrically-charged wire to make struts or even an entire chair in a single piece. Obvious polymer candidates, such as polyethylene terephthalate, failed to set in the intended manner, even when tested across a range of temperatures, setting times and intensities. But these experiments led Hendry and Choi to the realization that the size of the granules would play a significant role in the material's characteristics.

'We experimented for nearly two years, working with wax, water and shredded plastic,' says Hendry. 'None of these materials gave us the outcome we wanted, even though plastic felt like it had the most potential. We began using a combination of sand and powdered plastic granules – a mixture we saw being used at aluminium casting plants.'

When initial experiments with fine nylon and polyester powders had lumpy outcomes, they incorporated cristobalite sand. And when they discovered a source of dust-like nylon waste powder from the SLS 3D printing process and mixed it with sand, the pair had the result they had been looking for. 'The sand acts as a filler material as well as a heat conductor by distributing the heat around the wire,' the duo explains.

'The nylon powder melts and bonds during the curing process and turns the mixture into a solid body.'

With 3D printing now becoming commonplace, there is little prospect of a shortage of SLS nylon powder. The SLS process uses a laser to sinter powdered material, usually metal or nylon. By focusing the laser at points in space defined by a 3D model, the material is bound together to create a solid structure that is revealed when it is lifted out of the powder. Although effective, the process can be extremely wasteful. In the case of nylon SLS, some 44% of the composite is commonly discarded after production, even though almost half of it will be virgin nylon. Digits2Widgets, an architectural and engineering 3D model-maker in London, gave the duo a ton of nylon powder waste.

Using 1 mm nichrome wire, which they manually untwisted to remove curls and restore tension, Hendry and Choi created skeleton frames for a series of monobloc stools. The skeleton frames were placed in bespoke cuboid wooden boxes, through which the ends of the wire protruded so they could be reconnected to a power supply. The boxes were filled with the fine nylon and sand composite, and a 120-volt current passed through the wire heated the powder to around 500 degrees celsius (932°F). Most of the designs, including a cylinder suitable for use as vase, some small containers and the stools, which used various wire arrangements to create woven lattices, solid sections and thin legs, were created in less than half an hour, while diameters of up to 10 cm (4 in.) were achieved by leaving the electricity running for an hour.

After showing their work at the Royal College of Art graduate exhibition and the London Design Festival of 2016, Choi and Hendry were commissioned by Jeff Lincoln Gallery in New York to work on a redesigned collection of the 12 stools.

studio-ilio.com

Studio Ilio combine waste nylon from Selective Laser Sintering with sand to create a material that reacts to heat to become strong and durable.

Meijer subverts convention,
turning paper into wood
rather than wood into paper.
She glued sheets of surplus
newspaper together before
tightly rolling to create
a dense cylinder that, when
cut into, resembles wooden
logs. The remade material
can then be treated like
wood to produce furniture
pieces and surfaces.

NewspaperWood

Mieke Meijer

NewspaperWood had its genesis in 2003 when Mieke Meijer was a student at the Academy. Given the task of investigating wood, Meijer used newspaper surplus to reverse the traditional age-old process of turning wood to paper by returning newspaper to something that resembles its antecedent: wood.

Taking a stack of newspapers, Meijer meticulously glued each individual sheet to the next and rolled up the sheets into a tight cylinder. Like a log, the newspaper layers formed rings, just like the trunk of a tree. And when the 'log' was left to dry, the layers shifted and deformed, just like timber. Then, when a log of the material was cut into planks, the inks in the layers of paper emerged like wood grain or growth rings of a tree, reminiscent of the aesthetics of real wood.

This remarkable transformation appears to reverse the wood to paper process. To all intents and purposes, NewspaperWood looks like wood. It also behaves like wood – burning and twisting, cutting and wearing like wood. It can be cut, carved, routed, mortised, milled, nailed, sanded, painted and varnished – just like wood. It even burns like wood. But NewspaperWood is not wood, just a very effective trompe l'oeil that creates a convincing impression.

After graduation, Meijer abandoned further development of NewspaperWood until 2012, when in collaboration with Dutch design group Vij5, she returned to her invention. Now glued with an adhesive free of solvents and plasticizers, NewspaperWood has been turned from raw recycled material into a series of products in the form of lamps, jewelry and furniture including a desk, table, dresser and cabinet.

There are limitations. Larger sizes of NewspaperWood can be produced only as veneers because the size of the planks is limited by the maximum width of an open newspaper. The strength of the material depends on the strength of the glue. Although a non-organic adhesive would increase strength, the material would not be biodegradable. Meijer said that choosing an adhesive and plasticizers-free solvent enabled her to 'put our own sawing and sandpapering waste back into the circle, but also to bring the NewspaperWood products to the scrap yard for recycling'.

In 2014, Meijer and Vij5 experimented with using coloured newspapers, such as the salmon-coloured Financial Times, the yellow Italia Oggi and the pink La Gazzetta della Sport, all of which produced distinctive NewspaperWood samples with an interesting visual impact. However, in spite of its success as a new upcycled material, Meijer's creation faces an uncertain future. With newspapers moving from print to online, there is a very real possibility that Meijer's raw material might disappear and NewspaperWood could follow its progenitor into extinction.

newspaperwood.com

This page:

Wiltenburg proposes a future
in which precious metals can
be harvested from disused
electronic goods in the
city and recycled at home.
Salvaged aluminium could
be reforged using a micro-
domestic furnace.

Opposite:

The designer also
experimented with
weaving copper wire
mined from cabling.

Micro Urban Mining

Jorien Wiltenburg

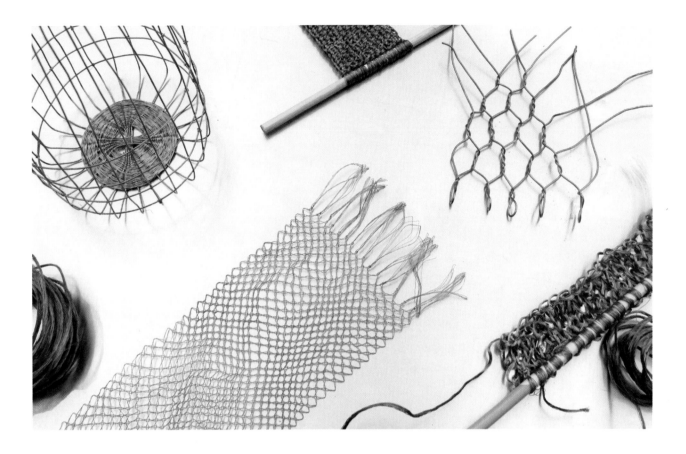

Electronic waste is one of the fastest-growing waste streams of the 21st century, and one with a particular paradox. Around 10% of global gold production and a third of silver goes into electronics, yet at a time of ballooning precious metal prices, less than a fifth of the 50 million tons of e-waste created globally each year is recycled.

With ever-increasing demand for next-generation electronic devices, e-waste mountains are threatening to overwhelm the planet and poison our future. In Guiyu, a city in China considered the world's e-waste capital, some 4,000 tons is dumped every hour (most likely explaining why it has the highest-ever recorded level of dioxin pollution and why 90% of its residents have neurological damage).

There is a potential fortune to be found in the heat sinks, transformers, cables, hard drives, components and circuit boards that make up most e-waste mountains. According to one estimate, they harbour gold and other precious metals in concentrations 40 to 50 times higher than in ores mined from the ground.

While conventional urban mining addresses the waste from building and industrial processes, Micro Urban Mining seeks to encourage individuals to recycle their own waste at home. Developed by Jorien Wiltenburg, a recent design graduate from the Willem de Kooning Academy in Rotterdam, Micro Urban Mining is a concept that she concedes 'is an intensive and time-consuming process for the individual,' but one which offers 'the satisfaction of doing it yourself'.

The process starts with disassembling computers and stripping cables to mine aluminium and copper. 'Looking at the properties of aluminium, the urban miner can melt this with meagre resources,' says Wiltenburg. She suggests that a home foundry can be constructed from common household items. A furnace could be 'made out of an old trash can poured with concrete'.

As for copper mined from cables, it 'lends itself well to be used in its solid form through various weaving techniques,' says Wiltenburg. 'This low-tech crafts work is in line with the self-sustaining approach of the urban miner. Restoring the connection between the creation and the use of an object gives us the strange but exciting feeling of having brought back to life something that was considered obsolete. Learning the skills needed for this process will restore the connection between creating and using an object.'

jorienwiltenburg.nl

Precious Plastic
Dave Hakkens

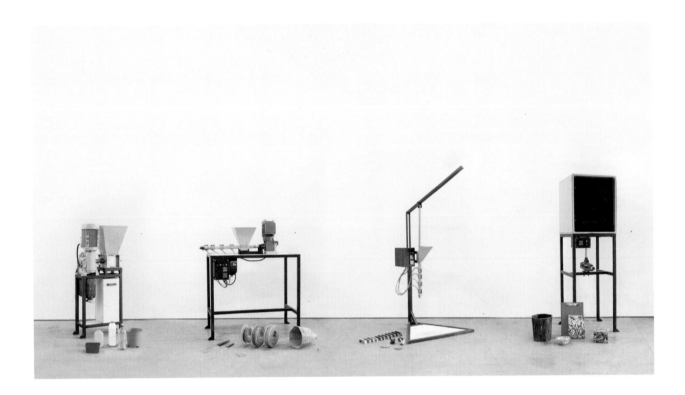

We're now living the future as Mr McGuire envisaged it in the iconic 1967 film The Graduate. 'I just want to say one word to you,' McGuire said, taking aside Benjamin Braddock, played by Dustin Hoffman. 'Just one word. Are you listening?' Hoffman nodded. 'Plastics.'

Plastics now dominate the planet, but not in the way Mr McGuire and his beloved wonder material's most ardent promoters envisaged. Made to last forever, but widely used in products designed to be imminently discarded, plastic has wheedled its indestructible, invidious way into every nook and cranny of the planet. Of the 311 million tons of plastic waste generated each year, less than a tenth is recycled, which prompted Dutch designer Dave Hakkens to develop 'a solution to the plastic pollution' that he calls Precious Plastic.

'The big plastic industry prefers to work with new plastic,' says Hakkens. 'Recycled plastic might slow down production or damage their machines.' So Hakkens developed a complete build-it-yourself home recycling system for the pernicious material. 'With wood or metal, you can recycle it yourself,' he says, but unfortunately not until now for plastic. The first of his four Precious Plastic appliances chops and shreds clean plastic refuse into scraps that can be used in the other three machines. The output size of the plastic flakes can be controlled by changing the sieve inside the machine and the flakes are then squeezed into filaments for 3D printers, or injected into a mould to form small objects, or compressed to make larger items.

Hakkens has used his Precious Plastic machines to make chopping boards, bowls, clipboards, plant pots, an injection-moulded spinning top, a lamp and a waste-paper bin, but says the processes could be adapted to make a wide variety of different products.

In the spirit of the open-source movement, Hakkens has made blueprints, instructional videos and directions for making his machines freely available online. Using scrap material to build the machines should limit costs to no more than £175 and take up to five days. 'We will teach you all the basics to get started, how to separate different plastic types, build your own machines, the best ways to collect plastic, templates to download and much more,' he says. 'By using basic materials, tools and universal parts, the machines can be built all over the world. Once you've built them you are ready to start a little recycle factory. Good luck!'

preciousplastic.com

Left and below:

These machines are rudimentary plastic moulding processing apparatus that allow users to recycle waste plastic into new products.

Opposite:

Hakkens has published a range of open-source machinery designs intended to be able to be built by anyone using materials readily available in any city in the world.

Pedros repurposes thrown-
away plastic bottles into
a joining mechanism for
future pieces. Through
low-fi heat processing using
a hand-held heat gun the
plastic melts around pieces
of wood to create a firm
stable bond. The designer
is teaching her methods at
workshops in London so that
others may find purpose for
plastic bottle waste.

Joining Bottles
Micaella Pedros

Joining Bottles, developed by London-based social and humanitarian designer Micaella Pedros, is the epitome of the aphorism that every now and then someone has an idea that is so simple and straightforward that its biggest wonder is why no one thought of it before. Realizing that plastic shrinks under the application of heat, Pedros has repurposed the drink bottles that plague the urban environment into a tool for joining pieces of wood.

'I was experimenting with resin from pine trees, developing the concept of native technology based on typical local materials,' she says. 'While I was pouring the heated resin onto various materials, I decided to pour the resin onto a plastic bottle. Impacted by the heat of the resin, the plastic started to shrink. At the time I was also finishing a project related to joinery, so at that moment it all just clicked.'

Pedros explains that 'following that spark, I explored the idea of using plastic bottles as a bonding material, developing the Joining Bottles technique by understanding its limits and possibilities through making.'

Joining Bottles involves cutting a ring of plastic from a bottle, wrapping around the junction between two pieces of wood, then warming it to 300 degrees celsius (572°F) with a heat gun. 'The strength of the joins depends on the grooves made in the wood,' says Pedros. 'The deeper they are, the stronger the join. It allows us to build functional structures, such as furniture, or to increase the length of timbers by joining offcuts together, or to repair furniture.'

Showcased in the Royal College of Art's degree show in 2016, Joining Bottles piqued interest particularly among children. 'People were really excited about the technique,' says Pedros. 'There is something quite satisfying and magical about it. Everyone encounters plastic bottles. Learning about a new way to make use of them inspires people to try it out themselves and it shifts our perspective on waste.'

Pedros has worked with R-Urban Wick, an urban resilience initiative based at Hackney Wick in east London. 'Because it is such an available and affordable technique with a strong potential of empowerment, I believe Joining Bottles is meant to be shared,' says Pedros, who has run workshops and plans to make her techniques open-source.

micaellapedros.com

Cochayuyo
by Sisa Collection.

2
Natural
Assets

—

Precious natural materials can be over-farmed and excessively cultivated, resulting in extreme depletion of natural ecosystems and the increase of by-product pollutants. Designers are acknowledging that the Earth's natural assets are a shifting landscape and what is abundant today may not be in the future. In order to reap sustainably, designers need to be flexible and inventive, basing their practice on what is currently available.

Since the proliferation of plastic in the 1950s, man-made and synthetic materials have dominated the design and product landscape. Speaking of modernity, these engineered materials promised durability and longevity, qualities that in light of current environmental concerns are perhaps less desirable than previously thought.

Natural materials and organic matter have once again become the ingredient of luxe design and an indicator of good quality. However, this shift from synthetic to natural brings with it another set of eco concerns – over farming. In order to satiate our desire for materials that are all at once natural and non-damaging, designers and makers are looking to discover new systems of resourcing.

Designers are exploring alternative raw materials and revisiting the planet's natural assets in order to develop sustainable solutions. They are farming naturally affluent crops such as seaweed or repurposing resilient resources that have fallen out of fashion. Makers are realizing that what was once an abundant resource may not be today and equally what is abundant today may not be in the future. As a result, they are thinking outside the box and allowing supply to inform demand as opposed to the other way around. They are replacing conventional natural resources such as cotton and cashmere with previously un-thought of, currently abundant alternatives, such as seaweed and yak fibre wool.

Alternatively, they are integrating circularity into existing agriculture. Through exploiting the organic 'waste' or by-product matter produced in various farming practices and natural ecologies, designers and makers are <u>Sweating the Resources</u> we already have access to. They are stripped of every leaf and branch, all sap and resin until not even a pine needle goes to waste. Through rudimentary, mainly mechanical experimentation, these new resources are transformed into viable environmentally friendly alternatives for new and existing applications in the design world.

Designers are increasingly looking backwards in order to design forwards. Revisiting the planet's forgotten natural assets, makers are reassessing the value of <u>Alternative Abundance</u> and ubiquitous raw materials such as seaweed and algae in order to develop organic alternatives to contemporary synthetics. Others are revisiting nature to hunt out unconventional harvests and are drawing from naturally abundant ecologies. Paying attention to the shifting currencies of the Earth, designers are acting with agility and allowing their practice to follow supply, rather than applying yet more pressure to already stretched conventional crops. Many are currently looking to the sea as a potential future farmland and harvesting from the wealth of seaweed and algae that grow unattended and unfettered in submerged vertical plantations.

Alternatively, designers are looking into the <u>Bio By-products</u> of existing agriculture to find function in waste and elsewhere, reassessing once-affluent industries to reposition resilient renewable resources that are lacking demand.

In their pursuit for a better future relationship with materials, designers are not creating new material industry but rather hitching a ride on existing cultivation and agriculture. They are striving to make existing systems more economically, environmentally and socially sound as they make strides towards a future of circular agriculture, zero waste and 100% resource optimization. They are working harmoniously with natural ecologies to build relationships that are symbiotic, not parasitic.

1

2

3

4

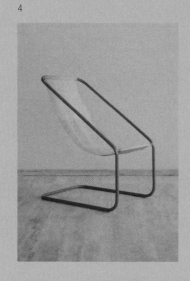

5

6

7

8

9

Sweating the Resources

Designers are adopting nose-to-tail and 'root-to-leaf' mantras. They are finding ways to utilize every element of harvested flora and fauna by applying unexpected processes and techniques.

1 — Forest Pine Wool by Tamara Orjola
2 — Reconfiguration of a Tree by Thomas Vailly
3 — Willow Project by Iceland Academy of the Arts

Alternative Abundance

For centuries we have relied on the same natural resources and have farmed and mined them to the point of near extinction. Naturally resilient crops are coming to the fore as alternative sustainable resources and designers are adopting ingenious ways to engineer these for a variety of applications.

4 — Sea Me Collection by Studio Nienke Hoogvliet
5 — Terroir by Jonas Edvard and Nikolaj Steenfatt
6 — Cochayuyo by Sisa Collection

Bio By-products

By-products of agricultural industries that would otherwise go to waste are being put to good use. These excess materials are transformed into biodegradable substitutes for contemporary polluting synthetics.

7 — Cornspan and From Chiang Mai by Apilada Vorachart
8 — Solidwool by Justin and Hannah Floyd
9 — From Insects by Marlène Huissoud

Julia Lohmann

Julia Lohmann, professor
of design at the University
of Fine Arts, Hamburg, and
director of her own design
practice, investigates
and critiques the ethical
and material value systems
underpinning our relationship
with plants and animals.

One of the biggest ailments of our society is that we've become blind to the value of the material we surround ourselves with. Look at anything around you, a plastic bag, for example, and think of what went into bringing it to you: millions of years of sedimentation transformed into plastic, into something we use for five minutes. I find it very sobering. Craftsmen are acutely aware of that value, of the natural history of their materials. The voice of the material coming through in the object is often very much appreciated in craft – and, while it is valued in craft techniques, it is almost impossible to achieve in industrial production and mass manufacture.

This whole idea of throwing things 'away' – 'away' doesn't exist. An item that falls out of cycles of use doesn't go 'away'; it renders the place where it ends up unusable – a landfill site, a river that stops fulfilling its function. There is no such thing as throwing 'away'.

As a designer, you are an amplifier, so you have a much bigger impact than any single consumer. Consumer choices have an impact, but a designer amplifies, whether they make many pieces or just one for a particular show. As a designer, you have a moral obligation to consider the impact of what you're doing.

Abundance is a term I would like to reframe. Aldo Leopold commented: 'We abuse land because we regard it as a commodity belonging to us. When we see land as a community to which we belong, we may begin to use it with love and respect.' Once you have a circular viewpoint, you realize everything is connected, and every time there is a linear progression that doesn't turn back, it becomes clear that there is a mistake. What is abundance? A kelp forest is an amazing natural resource – but it's abundant because we haven't used it. If we grab it as we have grabbed everything else, it won't be abundant anymore. When we look at resources we have to understand them in a different, more thorough way.

Asset is another term I find troublesome. I understand why we have to use these words – to make the value of nature apparent on the spreadsheets we run this world by, but, at the same time, the language is symptomatic of where we go wrong in the first place. We measure with entirely humancentric, short-term metrics, rather than biocentric, long-term ones.

GreenWave, a vertical ocean farm in Connecticut that won the 2015 Buckminster Fuller Challenge, aims to restore rather than deplete the ocean. Fish farming is an old paradigm. But how do we make it clear that we shouldn't eat certain fish? If we now have to eat seaweed and mussels instead of salmon, we can't order people to do that, so how do we make it desirable? That's where design becomes amazing. Many designers are frustrated by having to do things they don't believe in, but we can have a positive impact, we can rebalance.

We can definitely make things work: I don't agree, for instance, that we have too few resources to feed everyone – but we are so wasteful. We need to focus on positive examples, on things that work. Even small local projects can be scaled up. Ezio Manzini refers to 'cosmopolitan localism' – sharing knowledge and adapting it to local contexts. I think that massive change is inevitable. And we have the choice between massive change that we kick off, where we actively decide which things we really care about, and which we can let go. Or we run into change that is imposed upon us, and this would be a disaster.

Orjola found a way to turn
usually discarded pine
needles of the pine timber
industry into a textile
fibre. The designer used
the fibre to create solid
fibreboard furniture pieces
and carpets.

Forest Pine Wool

Tamara Orjola

Wood is one of the most desirable, versatile and prolific natural resources currently utilized. And, although in recent years great strides have been made in the preservation and replenishment of woodland ecology, we are still consuming more trees globally than we plant.

Pine is the most common tree species currently grown, 45% is grown in industrial man-made forests. In fact, 600 million pine trees are felled each year in the European Union alone and yet 20 to 30% of the total tree mass is left unused in the form of abandoned and shed pine needles on the forest floor. Inspired by this fact, Latvian designer Tamara Orjola began research into potential applications for the as yet untapped resource. She discovered that pine that had historically been utilized in food and herbal remedies is now only considered commercially for timber.

Through rudimentary material manipulation and manufacturing techniques such as crushing, soaking, steaming, carding, binding and pressing, the designer discovered that the needles could be transformed into paper and textiles, while harvesting essential oils and dyes in the process. Orjola's Forest Pine Wool experiments culminate in a library of material samples and a collection of stools and carpets composed entirely of pine needles.

What began as research into the forgotten value of plants, as well as the craft techniques and applications that have been lost in the wake of mass-production domination, has resulted in a proposal for an alternate, more sustainable attitude to pine. 'Proper consumption of the whole tree could reduce demand on other natural resources as well as the tree itself,' explains the designer. This endorses a root-to-leaf attitude in utilizing the waste matter of an already harvested resource, but also the ultimate products are 100% biodegradable.

Orjola believes that this way of thinking could greatly benefit large-scale design and production companies that make up the majority of timber consumers. This would create a much more holistically sustainable timber industry.

tamaraorjola.com

Reconfiguration of a Tree
Thomas Vailly

Since midway through the 20th century, synthetic resins and plastics have been prolific in mass production and fast-moving consumer goods. Many of these substances are themselves substitutes for material resources we traditionally procured from the natural world. Designers such as Vailly are beginning to reverse this usurpation by revisiting historical techniques and going back to the basic building blocks of the natural world.

Reconfiguration of a Tree celebrates the potential of bio-based materials with particular reference to the Pinus pinaster (maritime pine) tree, which grows in Mediterranean Europe. Believing that in the face of abundant and cheap synthetic material we have been overlooking the potential of natural resources, Vailly wanted to highlight the basic material compositions of the tree and illustrate how these multiple raw materials can be used as building blocks for new design processes and products. The Pinus pinaster is a resinous tree primarily harvested for its pitch. The studio experimented with the tree's material components, such as pine wood and black resin. The aim was to develop a range of man-made products that forgo any heavy chemical processing and the use of synthetic materials in favour of Pinus pinaster

ingredients that are low grade, renewable and biodegradable. The felled pine was, according to Studio Thomas Vailly, 'ripped apart' and its inherent material make up, including cellulose, lignin and rosin, rearranged with as few modifications as possible into rudimentary man-made substances. Vailly defines the result as an, 'abstraction of the tree', a collection composed of black resinous binding material and contrasting pale pine wood. Through collaboration with designers David Derksen, Gardar Eyjólfsson and Lex Pott, various products were developed to demonstrate the potential of the Pinus pinaster. Alongside a wealthy library of material samples, the collection included clogs, large and small furniture pieces such as screen dividers, tables and even toy boats.

By going back to the biological building blocks of nature, Studio Thomas Vailly hopes to promote the substitution of forgotten resources.

vailly.com

This page:

The studio collaborated
with various designers
to find applications for
the alternative natural
materials harvested from
the Pinus pinaster tree.
Lex Pott designed Clogs,
while Gardar Eyjólfsson
created a furniture piece
titled Exercise in Pine II.

Opposite:

Studio Thomas Vailly
researched the potential
of the Pinus pinaster
(maritime pine) to develop
a library of material samples
harvested from the tree.

This page:

The leftover tinted willow water was then boiled down to create dyes and pigments.

Opposite:

The team behind the Willow Project concentrated on techniques that used heat and water to discover alternative material resources within the tree. Boiling was used to loosen the bark and soften the fibres, enabling string and papermaking.

Willow Project
Iceland Academy of the Arts

The Willow Project by a collective of students from the Iceland Academy of the Arts saw the designers pushing the willow tree to its limits.

Centring in on the Salix genus, which consists of around 400 species of trees and shrubs, the designers collaborated with The Icelandic Forestry Association to explore the unknown potential of the tree. The willow was introduced to Iceland in around 1900 in an attempt to establish organized forestry and has had a rich role in Icelandic cultural heritage. However, historically it has not been considered a valuable resource and has mainly been used to cultivate soil in preparation for the growing of other plants.

Through experimental, deconstructive and transformative techniques, the design team discovered a variety of new material applications ranging from dyes and glues to paper, string and even fragrance. The aim of the project was to push the tree to its limits and explore its unknown potential.

The design team focused on rudimentary mechanical manipulations and the transformative power of heat and water-based processes such as peeling, splitting, smashing, burning, boiling and distilling to procure unexpected design materials.

Boiling was used to soften the fibres of the willow bark and leaves in order to enable string and papermaking. The leftover tinted willow water was then boiled down to thick black paste suitable to be used as glue. Along the journey from water to glue, the fluid passed through a gradient of rich reddish shades, leading the team to push experiments into willow-based pigments for dyes and coating. Burning also became a tool as the designers looked to ancient techniques such as the Japanese Shu-sugi-ban, a method of charring a wooden surface before cooling and cleaning it to create a natural protective coating. In the production of willow-wood charcoal, the designers found additional potential in the by-product. The ash produced in the burning process was found to be a useful source of salt, calcium carbonate and lye.

A key motivation behind the restricted treatments was the idea that the resulting materials will fit into a cyclical economy. Coming from nature they will go back into nature post useful life, leaving no synthetic or un-biodegradable matter behind.

'We were seeking to obtain a natural circulation of matter, to produce a counter example to our throwaway society. Everything we made had to be revertible to the forest as nutrition, but only after it had served another purpose.'

lhi.is

Sea Me Collection

Studio Nienke Hoogvliet

Studio Nienke Hoogvliet has been conducting ongoing research into the potential of seaweed as an alternative to conventional thirsty, polluting and space-greedy crops. As the realization that the production of textiles is an extremely polluting industry hits home, designers are looking for alternative crops that do not require excessive amounts of water and fertilizer, and equally do not leave a negative impact on the natural ecosystem. Creatives are looking for prolific material resources from naturally abundant ecologies as alternatives for the likes of cotton.

Naturally occurring, prolific and economical on space and external water and nutrients, seaweed is naturally detoxifying as it cleans the ocean of pollution such as phosphates. It is also one of the Earth's main sources of oxygen.

Not only has the designer developed a sustainable yarn derived from the plant, but she has also explored the vast alternative uses for the resource. A key discovery has been the spectrum of natural dyes that can be extracted from the weed. Shades, ranging from the expected browns and greens to greys, pinks and purples, can be procured from the different species of seaweed. Studio Nienke Hoogvliet worked on creating a circular, zero-waste process that would enable total optimal use of the resource. The waste of one process being fed into the next until none of the material remained.

To best exhibit the potential of her seaweed material developments, Hoogvliet designed a furniture collection including a chair and table. The seat of the chair is hand woven in seaweed yarn and dyed by the natural seaweed pigments. The leftovers of these processes can be used to create a paint for the tabletop, the waste again repurposed to make bio-plastic bowls.

nienkehoogvliet.nl

Left:

Colour samples of natural seaweed dye. Through ongoing research into the potential of seaweed, Hoogvliet discovered that spectrums of coloured dye could be procured from different types of seaweed. These dyes in turn would have a different effect depending on the different types of fibre treated.

Opposite:

Hoogvliet collected bladderwrack seaweed washed up on the shore in the Oosterschelde area of the Netherlands.

Below:

The Sea Me chair. The
seating is woven by hand
out of naturally dyed
seaweed yarn.

Opposite:

The seaweed-dying process.

This page:

Edvard and Steenfatt harvest seaweed that has been washed up along the shore of their native Denmark in large quantities.

Opposite:

The seaweed is hung to dry.

Terroir
Jonas Edvard and Nikolaj Steenfatt

Based in Denmark, Jonas Edvard and Nikolaj Steenfatt began their project Terroir as an investigation into local materials. The project title comes from the term used to describe the cultural and geographical relationship between products and the whereabouts of their production. The emphasis of their initial research was on highlighting the value in the considered provenance of raw materials. A value and consideration that is lost in the globalization of contemporary resourcing and manufacture.

Looking to what was abundant in their local environment, the designers began investigating the potential of seaweed. While some designers and innovators consider organized cultivation of the weed by way of offshore, submerged vertical farms, Edvard and Steenfatt utilized the plant as it naturally occurs, washed up on shore in large quantities.

The designers worked with the seaweed to produce a biodegradable material composite for durable furniture pieces. They harvest the seaweed from vast amounts washed up on shore and hang it to dry out. The dried seaweed is then ground down into a powder and cooked until it turns into a glue (a natural alginate found in the plant). This is combined with recycled paper to create a mouldable pulp, which is applied by hand to a mould and hardened to create a range of furniture pieces including lampshades and chairs.

The pair proposes that once the furniture has outlived its usefulness it can be broken down and reused or alternatively recycled as a natural fertilizer. This creates an entirely circular system. The aesthetic and textural qualities of the material vary in quality and colour depending on the species, again reinforcing the idea of aesthetic quality and provenance being intertwined.

jonasedvard.dk — steenfatt.dk

NATURAL ASSETS

This page:

The aesthetic and textural aspects of
the material vary in quality and colour
depending on the species.

Opposite, above:

Once the seaweed is dry it is ground down
into a powder and cooked and combined with
recycled paper to create a mouldable pulp.

Opposite, below:

The Terroir collection includes lampshades
and a chair composed of biodegradable
seaweed composite material.

This page:

The sliced seaweed is cut
into strips, adhered together
and shaped into a garment.

Opposite:

Cochayuyo, also known as bull
kelp, is the dominant species
of seaweed found in Southern
Chile. In its natural wet
state it is gelatinous and
elastic. When dry, a cross
section shows a hard exterior
skin with a spongy interior.

Cochayuyo
Sisa Collection

Chilean brand Sisa Collection has developed a project exploring the potential of cochayuyo, also known as bull kelp, which is the dominant species of seaweed found in Southern Chile.

The designers tasked themselves with questioning the materiality of fashion and realized that desirable materials in design are often foreign or rare. They chose to counteract this status quo by sourcing a locally ubiquitous raw material that was neither in short supply nor in high demand.

Cochayuyo is currently harvested and exported as a food ingredient and supplement, as it is known for its nutritional and healing properties. Sisa Collection worked with local supplier Herbamar to develop a handmade 'experimental skin' from the cochayuyo seaweed. The designers worked with the material in its natural state, adhering cut strips side by side to create a sheet. The seaweed is soaked to make it gelatinous and elastic and then shaped and moulded to take the form of the garment. The dried material holds its shape, the exterior skin of the

seaweed strips harden over a spongy interior to create a cushioning effect. The designers wanted to investigate alternative environmentally friendly resources, and push the limits of the abundant Chilean cochayuyo. However, although they are proposing the seaweed as a sustainable alternative resource, they are conscious about building a positive relationship with the natural ecosystem from the outset. They explained that although cochayuyo is plentiful, and very easy to harvest, it is also of paramount importance that the extraction of the algae is done with responsibility and measure, as although it is currently abundant it is not infinite and must be cared for and preserved.

sisacollection.com

Above and left:

The corn husks are
boiled with the ash of
household waste in order
to create extra fibres.
Charcoal from corn hobs
is added to the fibres
to aid moisture and
odour absorption.

Opposite:

Rice cultivation in
Thailand produces vast
amounts of organic waste
material in the form of
inedible corn husks.

Cornspan and From Chiang Mai

Apilada Vorachart

The environmental issues in agriculture do not only lie with wasted material but also with the disposal of this waste and by-product matter.

Easily cultivated and low maintenance, rice makes up the main food crop in Thailand. In Chiang Mai, Northern Thailand, the by-product material of this agriculture builds up to create huge mountains of waste matter and the isolation of the region means that it is difficult and expensive for the farmers to bring machinery in to clear this waste away. The corn kernels are used in animal feed but the corn husks and cobs currently have no purpose. It has become common practice to burn the waste, which results in an annual haze of air pollution. This in turn is hazardous to the health of the regions residents.

Inspired by this issue, designer Apilada Vorachart strove to reduce or even eliminate this air pollution by finding a material purpose for the corn waste. The project involved developing an economically attractive and environmentally friendly practice that would find a functional use for the waste while providing economic incentive for the farmers. Vorachart approached the challenge holistically to develop a proposal that is all at once financially beneficial, socially conscious and respectful of traditional craft skills of the region. Vorachart extracted fibres by boiling the corn husks with ash from household waste and borrowed local craft techniques and tools from an existing local papermaking industry to mould sheet material. The project led to the development of Cornspan, a new material derived from corn husk fibre ideal for the production of panels for sound and thermal insulation. The addition of charcoal from corn hobs is proposed for odour and moisture absorption.

The designer also considered the logistical implications of such an industrious expansion and designed the panels to be a quarter of the size of standard construction panels. This makes them easily transportable to local markets.

info.aplda@gmail.com

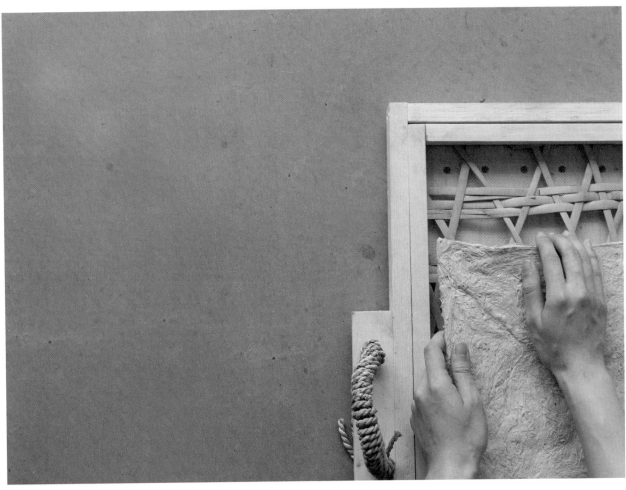

NATURAL ASSETS

Above and left:

A new material, Cornspan
is ideal for the production
of panels for sound and
thermal insulation.

Opposite:

Vorachart borrowed craft
techniques and tools from
an existing local papermaking
industry to mould the fibres
into a sheet material.

Herdwick wool, a by-product of
sheep farming traditionally
used in the British carpet
industry, is mixed with a
bio resin to create a fibre-
glass-like material suitable
for casting. Solidwool uses
the durable material to
create small home furnishings
and chairs.

Solidwool
Justin and Hannah Floyd

Solidwool is a development by Justin and Hannah Floyd that gives new purpose to Herdwick sheep wool originating from the Lake District.

Local industry relies on local material resourcing and globalization has led to some such industries falling short of demand. This shift is often at the detriment of not only traditional craft and manufacturing, but also local communities and economies. In the interest of sustaining these industries, designers and makers are reassessing resilient resources of dwindling industries and considering new applications or treatments.

Herdwick wool is wiry, dark and hard and is a by-product of sheep farming, typically used in the UK carpet industry. As demand for carpets has decreased the wool has been left unutilized. Solidwool is a unique composite material that combines the protein fibre with a bio resin where it acts as a reinforcing material not unlike fibreglass.

Wool is not considered a renewable resource, however, it is sustainable when responsibly farmed. The team is currently treating its Solidwool innovation as a medium for injection-moulded products, a sustainable alternative to today's petrochemical-based structural reinforced plastics. The Herdwick wool is combined with a bio resin that is roughly 30% renewable and sourced from waste streams of industrial processes such as wood pulp and bio-fuel production. The Solidwool collection thus far includes small home furnishings such as tablemats and coasters and larger-scale chairs. The Solidwool team is continually improving its process in pursuit of the most environmentally responsible manufacturing process and product line possible.

solidwool.com

From Insects
Marlène Huissoud

Designers and creatives are once again exploring what new precious materials can be procured from nature and existing ecologies. Glass and metals can linger in landfill and the processing and cultivation of luxe fashion materials such as leather and cashmere can have detrimental polluting effects on the environment. Clever manipulations of alternative natural matter could negate the need for harmful chemical intervention and waste.

Initially interested in the viability of using insects and their waste streams to create future craft artefacts, French designer Marlène Huissoud's research has included experimentations with by-products of bee-keeping and the waste of silkworms. This research has led her to develop a unique craft using propolis, a natural bee resin. Propolis has been utilized throughout history for its various inherent properties and believed healing quality. In Ancient Egypt it was even used in mummification to preserve bodies.

The biodegradable substance is composed of various tree resins collected by the honey bees that use it as a sealant within the hive. The colour and quality of the propolis is dependent on the amalgamated composition of tree resins. This gives propolis harvests from different geographical locations a specific identity. Huissoud chose to work with

black propolis, a substance rich in rubber-tree resin. Once heated and cleaned, this dense resin takes on a rich black tar-like consistency that solidifies with a high-shine finish, a glossy texture and natural fragrance. The designer experimented with the substance, employing various craft techniques and skills in order to establish its best potential behaviour. Discovering its resemblance to glass, the designer experimented with various glass craft methods including Venetian techniques, glass-blowing and engraving.

Propolis is biodegradable, but it is not an abundant material. As part of the existing bee-keeping ecology, it is harvested by the beekeeper around once a year and each hive will yield only around 100g of propolis in that period. The designer proposes the material as a precious yet biodegradable substance.

marlene-huissoud.com

Above:

Propolis is a natural by-product of bee-keeping and was treated to create a range of unique sculpted vases.

Opposite:

Huissoud investigated the potential of materials derived from insects' silkworm cocoons and natural bee resin to create silk paper.

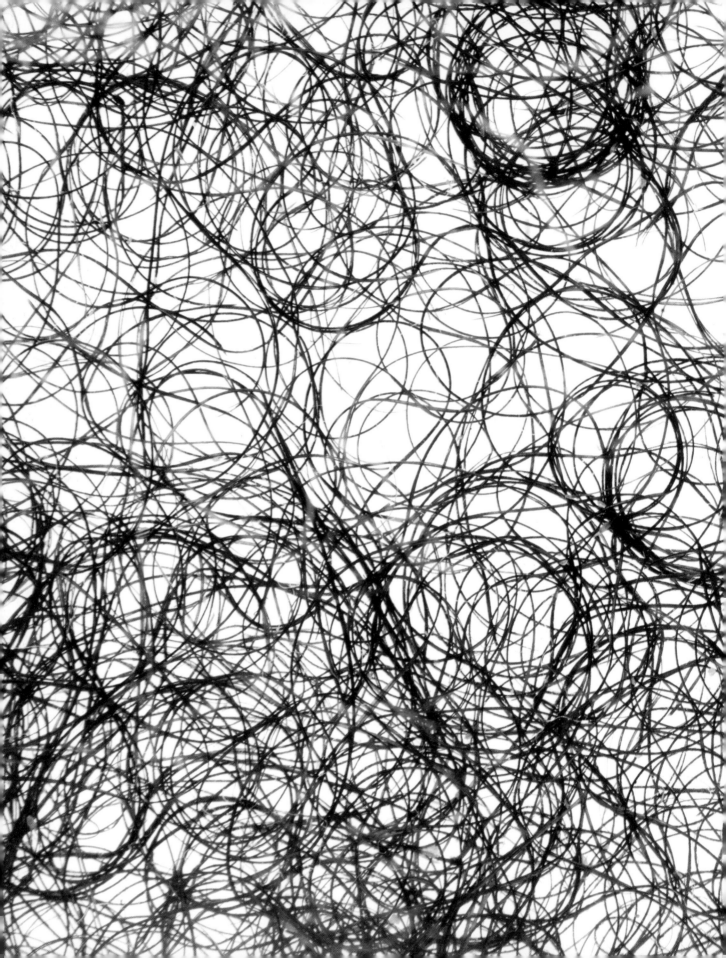

3
Shit,
Hair,
Dust

—

Human and animal biological waste is being explored as an abundant, sustainable source of exploitable material. Designers are challenging the negative connotations around shit, hair and dust, pushing the boundaries of renewable resources, and even challenging our perceptions of beauty.

With the world's population expected to exceed nine billion by 2050, shit, hair and dust generated by humans and the animals they keep are among the few natural resources whose abundance is increasing. As the population grows, so does the excrement and other biological detritus it generates: and this matter has the potential to be harvested, processed and exploited.

Designers, artists and scientists are all re-evaluating excrement and biological waste in all its guises, transforming materials with low perceived value to create not only functional products, but also beautiful items that transcend their humble origins. Faeces, hair and dust are coming to the fore as viable materials for future production.

In contemporary societies, shit is no longer used in design simply for its shock factor. Agricultural by-products are gaining favour for their renewability and abundant availability. Designers are exploring innovative ways to use manure as a sustainable source of both energy and materials such as biotextiles, plastics and building bricks. The UK alone produces around 110 million tons of organic waste each year and around 90 million tons of that is agricultural waste. Organic matter is easy to recycle, but when it is buried in landfill, it releases methane, a greenhouse gas, into the environment. Methane is in fact a valuable resource when correctly harvested, and can be used to generate power: our Museo della Merda case history is one example of this, as is the ZooShare biogas plant, which turns poo from Toronto Zoo and food waste from local grocery stores into renewable power for the citizens of Ontario.

Waste human hair, generally cut off and discarded, is showing new potential. This bountiful resource has high tensile strength, is a good insulator, and can be made into functional products such as cord, rope and netting. It can also be used as a design tool to create inks, patterns and delicate surface effects, or to produce exquisite artefacts and objects.

Making use of shit and hair is not without precedent. Historically, dung has long served as a fuel and a building material; animal hair has also been widely used in, for example, horsehair plaster, haircloth and upholstery. Dust, a mix of human and animal skin cells and hairs, pollen, textile and paper fibres and mineral particles, has never been associated with anything other than dirt and mortality. Designers today, however, are seeking out even this humblest of materials, using it as a design tool to create new composites for furniture and homewares, and even as a component of jewelry – making something precious and beautiful out of sweepings and dirt.

The projects explored in this chapter aim to challenge modern distaste for <u>Shit</u>, <u>Hair</u> and <u>Dust</u>, and open up a dialogue on sustainability, as well as promoting a message about a more healthy symbiotic relationship with the waste we produce.

1

2

3

4

5

6
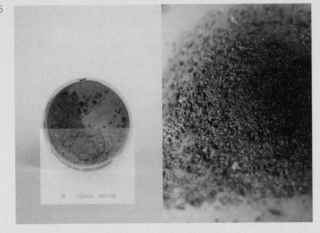

UK   LONDON   HOXTON

7
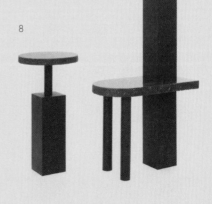

8

Shit

Excrement is a fundamental of existence; it exists in huge quantities and, as long as life on earth continues, is infinitely renewable. Harnessing the potential of shit has so far been largely confined to its traditional uses as a fuel, fertilizer and building material. Designers are now, however, taking a fresh look at the potential of poo.

1 — Merdacotta by Gianantonio Locatelli and Luca Cipelletti
2 — Mestic by Jalila Essaïdi

Hair

As long as the world is populated by humans, human hair will remain an abundant, easily available resource. Hair is strong yet biodegradable, and completely sustainable and natural. Designers are starting to recognize its unique (and perhaps surprising) potential in a variety of projects.

3 — The New Age of Trichology by Sanne Visser
4 — Hair Highway by Studio Swine
5 — The Colour of Hair by Fabio Hendry and Martijn Rigters

Dust

Dust must be one of the humblest materials on earth. However, 21st-century designers and makers are reinterpreting the detritus of our daily lives as a versatile material that can be used to make luxury furniture, jewelry and ceramics.

6 — Dust Matters by Lucie Libotte
7 — Dust by Ágústa Sveinsdóttir
8 — How Dust This Feel? by Matilda Beckman

Zoe Laughlin

Zoe Laughlin, co-founder and director of the Institute of Making and the Materials Library project, works at the interface of the science, art, craft and design of materials.

Disgust is very subjective. For example, when you buy copper, they don't tell you the story of the hundreds of people who died to bring it to you – copper mining is incredibly destructive. That could well be considered disgusting, though it doesn't elicit the same response as a product made out of poo. One solution is simply not to tell people. Using materials such as poo and hair to make beautiful stuff is in the design territory that actively seeks to open a conversation – and engaging in articulate design practice is great, of course! But if you are making bricks out of poo, you're not trying to win a design award, you're trying to produce something that can be used to make buildings. The people who use that building don't need to know what the bricks are made of.

There's always going to be a moment when you're doing something with a new material and the story of what you've done becomes part of the value of the made object. To make consumers want to pick your item, you want to tell them that story. But the ultimate goal is for consumers to pick that thing because it's a better thing, or simply because they like it. The material should become more in the background. Ultimately, in this particular context, you'd pick, say, manure because it's a great building material, not because you're making a conscious effort to pick it because of its story.

There is a time when a material has novelty value that will attract early adopters and raise awareness, but then the material should just become default, so people who choose it for other reasons don't necessarily need to know the story.

Lots of projects skirt the issue of scaling up. For example, you might see a project that uses perhaps waste fish scales, compressed into plastic-type material that can be used like other plastics. But there is a huge jump from individual small design projects to the big supply chains, to the stuff that gets made industrially.

I could see the use of this kind of waste becoming mainstream if the will was there. But the management of our waste as a species would have to be reinterpreted as a form of agriculture, on a large-scale akin to that of farming. At the moment it feels a bit niche. The will comes down to top-level legislation, and at the moment smaller-scale projects are being left to bubble up from the bottom. To work at a scale where the potential of our waste is realized would require action at a whole different level. I don't think it's the fact that our waste is disgusting that's stopping us; it's that we are used to dealing with it in certain ways. That is difficult to change, and would require a very complex new system.

Landfill sites are incredible places where objects disappear into the ground in the hope of disposing of them but these sites will become increasingly valuable as a mine for materials and a resource in the future. Unfortunately, crises tend to drive this kind of search for alternative sources. Making genuinely effective use of waste requires very long-term thinking.

Design is utterly central to helping solve some of the really big questions we're looking at here. For millennia, farmers were at the heart of every nation, providing the food we eat. In the future, designers could be equally important. If we consider designers as farmers of material, there is potential, excitement, opportunity. These issues are too big for any single nation and we need collaboration in the same way that nations have collaborated on CERN and the space project. We need a design strategy across our made world that isn't driven by a corporation or a single nation: we need to come together on a global level.

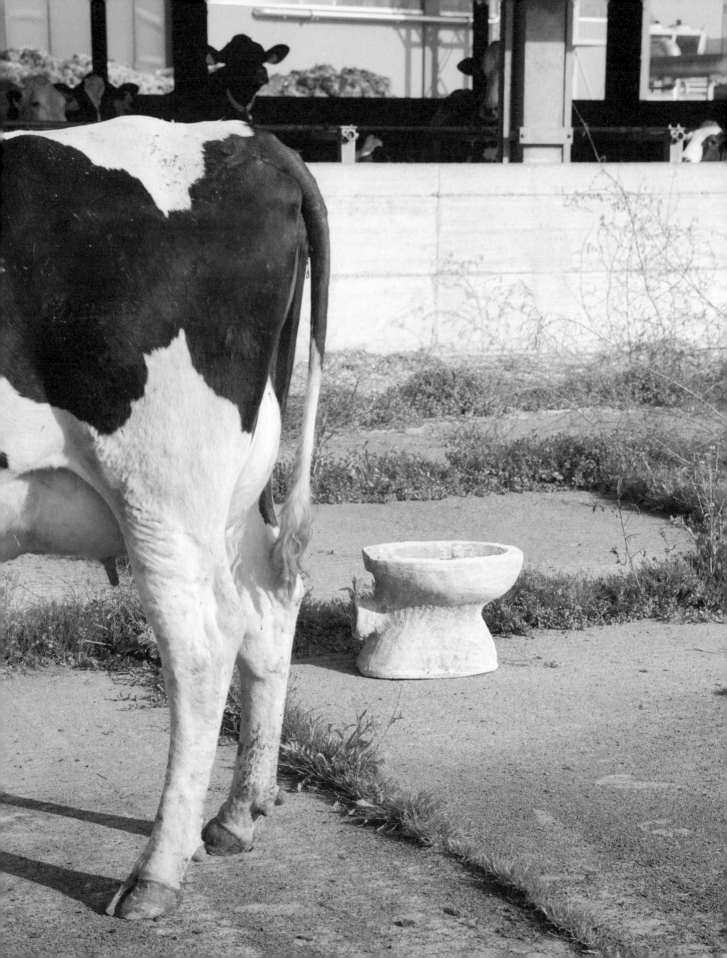

Merdacotta
Gianantonio Locatelli and Luca Cipelletti

The Museo della Merda (Museum of Shit) in Italy extracts maximum value from cow dung. Once the raw manure has been used to generate methane gas, the remaining material is used to make merdacotta, a clay composite made of processed dung. Merdacotta is currently used to create products such as tiles, pots, tableware and decorative pieces, but its potential could be considerably wider. Could sustainable merdacotta bricks one day be used to build houses? Dung in less sophisticated forms already has a long traditional history of usage as a building material in, for example, structures made of cob or of wattle and daub.

'The main idea that drives a revolution is transformation. We are using one of the poorest materials on Earth and not only using it, but more importantly transforming it, in numerous creative ways. We are giving a second life to a subject that has a low perceived value,' says agricultural entrepreneur Gianantonio Locatelli, who founded the Museo della Merda in Lombardy in 2015. The museum is housed in a medieval castle on the Castelbosco dairy farm, one of several owned by Locatelli; in total, every single day, his 3,500 cows produce not only around 50,000 litres of milk, but also around 150,000 kg (331,000 lbs) of dung. The milk is used in Grana Padano cheese, but the poo is proving just as productive. Since 2007, the Castelbosco farm has produced all its own electricity from manure-generated methane, and currently generates up to three megawatts of energy per hour. When the raw manure has been processed in a digester, the remains, mixed with clay and straw, are the base for merdacotta.

The Museo della Merda was designed not only as a place to showcase ideas and exhibitions (items on display include fossilized faeces and shit-based artworks), but also as a centre for concrete objects and projects; merdacotta symbolizes the sustainability that underpins the museum's principles. The design of items that bear the Museo della Merda brand is simple, clean and rural. This no-frills approach harks back to ancient principles which, says Locatelli, 'state that the substance is not in the shape but in the material they are made of. These are objects that redesign the cycle of nature in a virtuous circle.'

The Milano Design Award is an accolade presented to the top installation at Milan Design Week; Shit Evolution, curated by architect Luca Cipelletti, one of Locatelli's associates and business partners, took the Museo della Merda concept to Milan, and scooped the 2016 award. The judges praised a process 'capable of destabilizing common perceptions'. If a concept based on shit can win a top design award in Milan, surely future possibilities for excrement must be infinite.

theshitmuseum.org

SHIT, HAIR, DUST

This page:

Merdacotta challenges the common perceptions of excrement as a material for design. By mixing the excrement with straw and clay, it can be used to create products such as tiles, tableware and other decorative objects, but its potential could be considerably wider and even be applied to architectural projects.

Opposite:

The Museo della Merda transforms one the of poorest materials on Earth, excrement, into merdacotta, a clay-like material. Cow dung collected from the Castelbosco farm in Lombardy, Italy, is transformed into both energy and a material for making functional and decorative objects.

Mestic considers manure
as a valuable resource to
create sustainable bio-based
materials. It has developed
a way to turn the abundance
of cow excrement into
bioplastics, biotextiles
and biopaper.

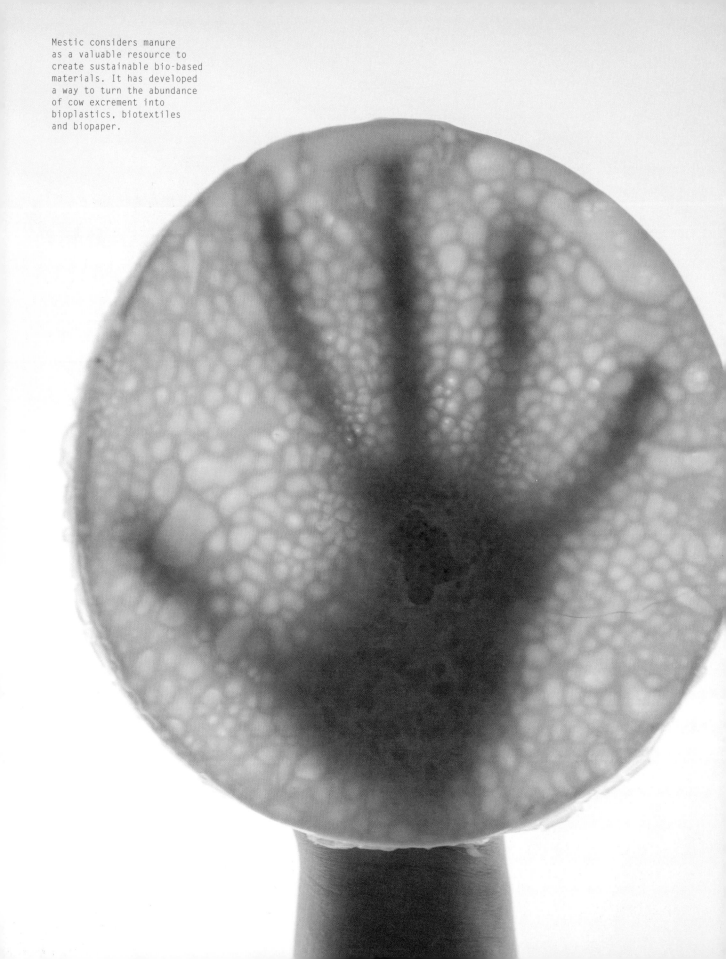

Mestic

Jalila Essaïdi

Mestic is the first (and, so far, only) company in the world to convert animal manure into biotextiles, bioplastic and paper. 'Mestic is all about transforming raw matter into future opportunities,' says Jalila Essaïdi, an artist and entrepreneur who works in modern technology and is the director of Inspidere, the Eindhoven-based biotech company behind Mestic.

In 2015, Mestic was approached by the agricultural sector in the Noord-Brabant province in the south Netherlands to seek a solution for the dispoal of surplus cow manure. Dutch farmers are having to curtail the amounts of manure their farms generate, due to international regulations over excess phosphate entering the environment; but they don't want to cut back on the number of cows they keep. The Mestic team developed a way to turn the manure into bioplastics, not only tackling the excess excrement, but also providing a sustainable source of biomaterials.

This, says Essaïdi, is the first time that the manure has been considered to be a valuable resource rather than simply a problem. 'In Germany, for instance, great advances have been made in the fermentation of manure into fertilizer; others have succeeded in turning manure into energy. Those are great initiatives, but they're not very efficient. And even at their peak performance, they are still only partial solutions. A true result would be to completely strip the manure and use the resultant cellulose to manufacture new, biomaterial products. And once you've made that step, you'll notice: manure is worth its weight in gold.'

Essaïdi focuses on the cellulose component of manure, repurposing it as usable and versatile plastic, textile and paper materials; the first fashion show featuring garments made from

Mestic biotextiles took place in June 2016. How is this amazing transformation achieved? The manure is treated at the farm of origin to extract the correct components, both solid and liquid. The fermentable components can also be extracted and used to manufacture the chemicals needed for pulping and acetylation, key parts of the production process. Pulping and acetylation turns the cellulose extracted from the solid components of the manure into high-grade cellulose pulp and bioplastic.

A scale-up of Essaïdi's current company will be established in the Moerdijk municipality in the Netherlands, where the first production lines will start manufacturing manure-based bioplastics, biotextiles and biopaper. Essaïdi also has her sights firmly set on even larger projects. 'The possibilities are endless. For instance, we are planning to build a bridge across the A2 motorway at Eindhoven Airport by 2021. The major difference between that project and our other products is that the bridge should not be biodegradable. That's something that needs fixing first!'

The establishment of a circular economy model, where materials are cyclically used, repurposed and recycled, has great potential for tackling worldwide problems such as resource scarcity, pollution and waste. Mestic's ultimate goal is to make a 'significant positive impact on global climate objectives. We are all here to make a serious contribution to a new, circular world.' The company takes its name from 'mest', the Dutch word for manure. As the company says: 'Manure matters.'

mestic.eu

Making plastic from the cow manure.

Natural fibres derived from the cow manure.

A solid piece of cellulose acetate derived from cow manure.

SHIT, HAIR, DUST

Textile made of dissolving grade cellulose derived from the natural fibres in cow manure.

A first attempt to make a transparent foil.

Hair has a high tensile strength, making it
perfect for use in yarn, rope and netting.
On average, one human hair can hold up
to 100 g (0.2 lb) of weight, depending
on the person's diet, health, environment,
ethnical background and treatment of the
hair. A whole head of hair could potentially
withstand a weight of 12 tons. Asian hair
growth is the fastest and the strongest.
When made into rope Asian hair can withstand
more weight than Caucasian hair.

The New Age of Trichology

Sanne Visser

Material researcher and designer Sanne Visser sees hair as a supremely practical design resource and has used it to create an array of utilitarian products such as rope, bungee cord and netting.

'Human hair is currently not considered as a useful fibre, even though there is an abundance of it and it has a very obvious sustainable production process compared to other natural fibres,' says Sanne Visser. The UK, she says, generates 'around 6,500,000 kg (14,000,000 lbs) of human hair waste annually, which mostly ends up in landfills.'

The New Age of Trichology diverts some of that hair into more useful channels. Visser gathers hair from London hairdressers and makes two-ply yarn from it, helped by professional spinner Diane Fisher, who managed to card the hair and spin it despite its relatively short lengths. To exploit hair's high tensile strength, Visser asked ropemaker and knot specialist Des Pawson to make the yarn into rope, which could then be fashioned into other items such as netting bags. Visser uses Asian hair, as it is stronger than either African or Caucasian hair; her two-ply ropes have a minimum breaking load of 32 kg (70 lbs). Once the rope products have reached the end of their useful life, they can be composted or recycled.

'This is just the beginning,' says Visser. The New Age of Trichology aims to further develop other techniques and materials focusing on different properties of hair, including thermal insulation, oil absorption and flexibility, and Visser hopes to collaborate with experts in fields such as agriculture, medicine, construction and engineering. She also hopes that projects such as hers, which draw on the traditional crafts of spinning and ropemaking, will help maintain such skills for the future: 'I hope that I can inspire other people to get to know the process of these crafts, where handmade and machine tie in.'

She is currently looking at ways to maximize production by creating open-source machines to replicate the carding, spinning and ropemaking processes. This is partly to speed up production and make it cheaper. Far from superseding the handcrafted element of the project, however, this will enhance it, says Visser. The open-source element means that anyone, anywhere in the world, will be able to work with human hair. 'This will not only reduce pressure on other non-renewable materials, but will also lead to more creative ideas and outcomes made from human-hair yarn and ropes. Makers and designers will be able to experiment with the yarn using their own skills such as knitting, crocheting and weaving, or explore different areas where it could be used.'

sannevisser.com

The New Age of Trichology
by Visser demonstrates how
human-hair waste streams
can be used to create new
materials. Hair gathered
from the floors of London
hairdressers is made into
two-ply yarn. The yarn is
then made into rope.

Collecting hair from a London hairdresser.

Professional spinner Diane Fisher making two-ply yarn from human hair.

Ball of two-ply yarn spun from Asian hair.

Ropemaker Des Pawson turning the hair yarn into rope.

Hair Highway
Studio Swine

Hair Highway by Studio Swine explores hair's potential as a natural composite.

By combining hair with natural resin, Studio Swine has created beautiful wood-like solid surfaces, with a tortoiseshell-style aesthetic and a grain that resembles exotic hardwood or polished natural horn – materials that are rare or endangered when sourced from trees or animals.

Azusa Murakami and Alexander Groves, the designers behind Studio Swine, developed the Hair Highway collection for Pearl Lam Galleries; the project was selected as a highlight at Design Miami/Basel and won a Wallpaper* award. The pieces in the collection, which include exquisite boxes, trays and combs, were inspired by items from the Qing dynasty and by the Shanghai-deco style of the 1920s and 1930s; their distinctive, elegant lines reflect the Chinese roots of the project. Murakami and Groves travelled to China to investigate the international hair trade based in the Shandong province; businesses in Shandong export human hair across the world, mainly for use in the beauty industry. Hair Highway explores far wider possibilities. Asian hair grows particularly quickly – up to 16 times faster than hardwood mahogany, according to the

designers, who also say a full head of hair is strong enough to take the weight of two African elephants. Murakami and Groves envisage the hair-based composite they have developed as a sustainable alternative to old-growth tropical hardwoods and exotic animal horn. China is the world's largest importer of tropical timber and also one of the world's main consumers of animal horn.

The Hair Highway collection is based around a central concept of the ancient Silk Road, which once transported not only silk, but also goods, technologies, aesthetics and ideas between East and West. Hair Highway reflects on China's new relationship with the rest of the world, while revisiting the idea that trade has the ability to transport values and perceptions as well as material goods.

studioswine.com

Studio Swine's documentation
of the human-hair trade in
Shandong province, China.

Studio Swine reimagines
hair as an abundant and
renewable alternative to
rare or endangered materials
sourced from trees and
animals. By combining hair
with a natural bio resin,
Studio Swine invent a new
composite material with
an exotic aesthetic that
evokes polished horn or
tropical hardwoods.

SHIT, HAIR, DUST

Vases in the Hair Highway
collection.

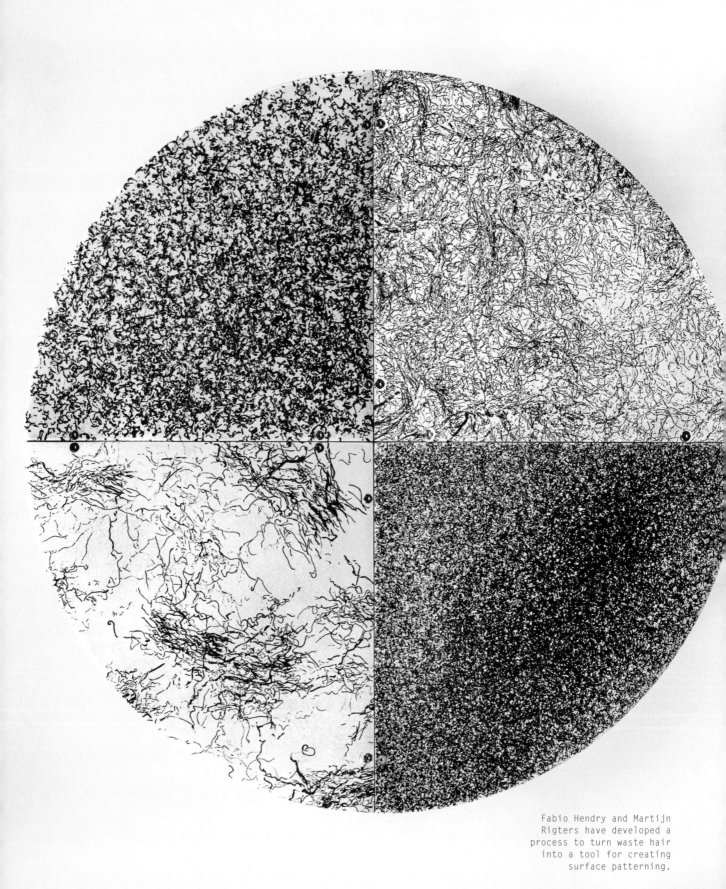

Fabio Hendry and Martijn
Rigters have developed a
process to turn waste hair
into a tool for creating
surface patterning.

The Colour of Hair
Fabio Hendry and Martijn Rigters

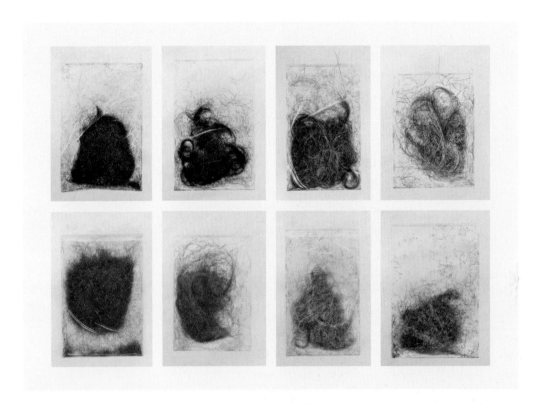

Fabio Hendry and Martijn Rigters have worked out how to turn hair into an ink that can be used on various metals, both as decoration and to create surface effects.

When the hair is applied to a hot surface under carefully controlled conditions, keratin, its main protein, carbonizes instantly, making a permanent, durable pattern. Hendry and Rigters, who met while studying design at the Royal College of Art in London, have experimented with various metal surfaces in the Colour of Hair project, and so far have achieved their best results on aluminium, which doesn't discolour when it is heated, and shows patterns well on its silver-white surface. The aluminium sheets are first sanded to achieve a matt finish, which amplifies the effect of the print, then placed in a specially adapted industrial barbecue grill where they are heated at 350 degrees celsius (662°F) for about 10 minutes. The hair is then applied to the metal, within 5 to 10 seconds – it's a precise process, as adding the hair too early causes fumes to penetrate the aluminium and leave impurities on the print, while applying it too late means it doesn't fully carbonize. The sheets are then slowly cooled and rinsed with water. Objects created so far include subtly finished attractive tables, beakers and trays.

The hair offcuts are sourced from hairdressers in London, and the designers have discovered they can create different patterns depending on the length of the original fibres: some look like hair, while others are more abstract. They are currently experimenting with other natural materials, including cat hair dislodged when the pet is brushed, and with different effects, including subtle contrasts created when ferrous metals are used; unlike aluminium, ferrous metals change colour when heated.

'We are also extending the application of the end product by printing on ceramic tiles and sheets,' say the designers. 'The process works similarly to aluminium; the clay is heated in an oven. Being able to print on any metal as well as on ceramics, we believe that we can cover a major part of interior application.'

thecolourofhair.com

When hair is applied to a hot surface under carefully controlled conditions its main protein, keratin, carbonizes instantly, creating a permanent, durable pattern.

SHIT, HAIR, DUST

Different patterns can be achieved, depending on the length of the original fibres and the ethnic origin of the hair. Some patterns clearly resemble locks of hair, others are more abstract speckles or have the appearance of marbled surfaces.

Designer Lucie Libotte wants to change
common perceptions of dust as dirty and
repulsive detritus into a material that
can be sourced to create unique ceramic
glazes. Depending on location, dust contains
different particles of organic, inorganic
and synthetic materials, so glazes vary
in colour and texture.

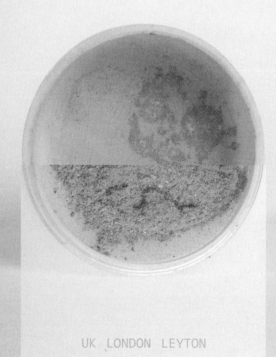

UK LONDON LEYTON

UK LONDON HOXTON

Dust Matters
Lucie Libotte

Materials designer Lucie Libotte uses dust as a way to tell stories. She makes house dust collected from homes in cities such as London, Dublin, Neumünster, Milan and Brussels into distinctive glazes for ceramic pieces. Depending on location, the dusts contain different particles of organic, inorganic and synthetic materials, so the glazes vary in colour and texture, revealing a new perspective on the location where the dust was collected.

'House dust is commonly perceived as dirty, intrusive and repulsive,' says Libotte. 'We know it as a fine grey powder consisting of tiny particles and waste matter, lying on surfaces or drifting in the air. It is in every room, in every house, in every country. We live among it every day and yet it is virtually invisible.' She says that sweeping away dust is sweeping away the past. House dust varies widely, explains Libotte, depending on the lifestyle activities of the inhabitants, their occupations,

the products they use, and their housekeeping practices. 'Dust is in essence the passage of time.' The surprisingly varied, subtly beautiful finishes on the ceramic objects she produces offer a unique narration of the geology, history and identity of the location where the dust was collected.

In a recent collaboration with ceramics maker and artist Irina Razumovskaya, the project experimented with different forms of ceramic vessel, looking ahead to shaping architectural pieces in the future. 'We hope to inspire a fresh perspective towards dust as we see many potentials in the material,' says Libotte.

lucielibotte.com

Ágústa Sveinsdóttir collects dust
from derelict buildings across
Iceland, including abandoned farms,
binding it using a biodegradable
adhesive, and using it to coat
metal rings and bangles. Her
jewelry questions if dust could
ever be a precious raw material?

Dust

Ágústa Sveinsdóttir

The Dust jewelry collection by Ágústa Sveinsdóttir reinterprets dust as a precious raw material, and in the process poses questions about material worth. 'We always demand that everything should be flawless but in the end, everything is dust or in time becomes dust. Is it possible to make use of materials that have always been considered nothing more than useless dirt?' asks the designer.

Sveinsdóttir gathered dust from derelict buildings across Iceland, including abandoned farms, bound it using a biodegradable adhesive, and used it to coat metal rings and bangles. The dust coating gradually wears away to reveal the structure of the jewelry beneath, making transformation and disintegration an integral part of the design.

'It is a celebration of the fragile beauty that time and use impart to materials,' explains Sveinsdóttir. 'In this world everything existing is linked to the process of birth, decay and disappearance. That is the way of life, the way of nature.

Inspired by the tradition of the symbolic vanitas paintings, the Dust collection is a reminder of the transience of all earthly pursuits and how it can be a motive for design.'

Dust was conceived as part of the 2014 Spiritualism, Craft and Waste series of projects by students graduating from the product design department of the Iceland Academy of the Arts. This graduate collection set out to question the role of the contemporary designer. 'It is a redefinition and revitalization of modern values: instead of focusing solely on the making of commercial merchandise, designers should start to question the impact of their work on other living systems,' says Sveinsdóttir.

behance.net/aaagusta

How Dust This Feel?

Matilda Beckman

Matilda Beckman's How Dust This Feel? collection of a table and chair is partially made from dust she has collected from the floors of vintage clothing shops.

The Sweden-based designer collects the dust from vacuum-cleaner bags and freely admits that, in its raw state, dust is 'gross'. However, by mixing it with a wood-glue binding agent and compressing, moulding and varnishing it, she transforms it into a finish that resembles stone or marble – with its own new beauty. The furniture, however, acknowledges its origins: while the table and seat top are richly lacquered, the unvarnished sides show the random fibres used as a raw material.

'We are running out of natural resources and yet the backbone of the world's economy is made up of consumerism. Tomorrow, all the things we now take for granted might not be here anymore. We shop on autopilot, leaving all trace of an afterthought in the dust,' says Beckman, who is based in Sweden. 'So dust is what I have used as a base when creating this environmentally friendly building material. I want to refine and display that which is usually found in the corners.'

studiobeckman.com

Matilda Beckman transforms
dust into a material that
resembles stone or marble,
reinterpreting the humble
detritus of our daily lives
into a desirable finished
product.

4
Material Connections

—

Designers are using materials and making as the means to drive social innovation. This ranges from establishing and maintaining communities to disseminating and sharing skills – it can even refresh our connections with tradition.

Transparency and provenance are key concerns in an age where information is readily available and it is increasingly hard to gloss over exploitation of the environment, of resources or of people. This is making everyone more mindful, including designers and makers – and their clients. It is affecting both the practicalities of material choices, and the way that designers consider their roles in terms of positive social impact.

Global outsourcing of production creates huge distances between designers, manufacturers and customers. This once made it easy to conceal horrific working conditions for workers tasked with material extraction and processing, particularly as increasing demand led to vastly increased production rates. However, a series of large-scale exposés means that no one can now claim ignorance of unsound practices. We are now far more aware of the social implications of our design decisions.

This increased knowledge of the impact of shifts in production is coupled with a new attitude to consumption. Customers in the developed world have recognized that it is possible to have too much 'stuff' – there is a widespread sense of 'stuffocation'. This has led many designers to adopt an approach in which social entrepreneurship and social engagement take on a new significance. Such designers are shifting their emphasis away from the function or output of products, and refocusing on empowering and enabling others, and on connecting and strengthening communities. This is supported by shifts in culture and values, and by a growing emphasis on the human dimension – on putting people first.

Social connection has long been acknowledged as a key component for physical and mental wellbeing. However, particularly in urban environments, neighbourhood communities are in decline; this is partly due to decreasing engagement with once ubiquitous social gathering points such as religious services, and partly due to funding being stripped from local services and amenities. The number of people living alone is rising across the world, meaning that finding ways to connect with others in our locale has never been more important.

Designers are recognizing this need and are looking to employ material manipulation and making as a way to facilitate social connection, nurturing a sense of community through shared participation. This can be a literal bringing together of people to work on a shared project, or it can be about connecting diverse groups of stakeholders to address a specific problem or issue.

Aware of the value of collaborative practice, designers who seek to use material as a method of connection are engineering scenarios, locally and internationally, in which people can exchange and share knowledge and ideas and, particularly, pool their skills. The de-skilling that stems from mechanized production has led to the marginalization of traditional craft communities, particularly in the developing world. We profile designers who have taken action, creating innovative partnerships with businesses and non-governmental organizations and with the artisans themselves, to empower individuals through the supply chain and support local communities.

The communal practising of making and crafting speaks to our desire for physical connection with material as well as with other people. In an increasingly technological world where so much of our activity is screen-based, using our hands for more than pressing buttons or clicking on links promotes a sense of agency, fulfilment and empowerment.

Material culture – the connection of humans to material and the way materials are processed into objects – has come to the fore. As a backlash against mass production, we are seeing a growing desire to preserve and celebrate material and craft tradition. In an age of industrialized production, we are drawn back towards the object as a vessel to tell stories and encompass narrative.

1

2

3

4

5

6

7

8

Connecting Communities

Materials and making are tools and processes that can bring people together. As these projects prove, working on a common undertaking with a common purpose generates and knits together groups and communities, engaging minds as well as hands.

1 — Breadline by Bethany Williams
2 — Granby Four Streets by Assemble
3 — FrankenToyMobile by Andrés Lemus-Spont, Marya Spont-Lemus,
Louis Fernandez and Michael Pecirno

Connecting Skills

Designers are gaining mutual benefit from sharing their knowledge and ideas locally, nationally and globally. This is a win-win situation: while facilitating a collaborative approach to solving problems, they are also enhancing their own skills, and ultimately creating a design community with no boundaries.

4 — Refugees Company for Crafts and Design by CUCULA
5 — Bottle-Up by Super Local in collaboration with Klaas Kuiken, OSΔOOS and StoneCycling

Connecting Tradition

In order to move forward, we rely on the work of others who have gone before; lessons learned in the past pave the way to the future. For some 21st-century design projects, this connection with heritage and tradition is particularly fundamental.

6 — Beyond the Mainland by Phoebe Quare
7 — The People's Brick Company by Something & Son
8 — Karawane by Pour les Alpes

Daniel Charny

Daniel Charny is director
at the From Now On creative
and cultural consultancy,
professor of design at
Kingston University, founder
and director of Fixperts,
and an honorary senior
research fellow at London's
Victoria and Albert Museum.

Sometimes engagement is for making and sometimes it's through making – there is a difference. For example, when the community gets together to build a barn, that's coming together for making. But if you set up a making project in a library in a challenged neighbourhood, get people to spend time together, connect with each other, connect with the library, the products they are making are less important in themselves. The more public a project is, the more it is about engagement through making. Both involve building community, authorship, pride and resilience.

This is important because it's not just about making things, it's about understanding that you are part of a community, part of a society. Connectivity and knowledge sharing are a way we can deal with complex problems in the world. There is a feel-good factor to sharing skills, a sense of altruism, but there's much more to it. Open data, open sources, open knowledge are the only way we're going to be able to face all kinds of very difficult situations: sustainability, economic problems, ecological problems, social care, immigration. All of them are about connectivity and empathy. If you experience a relationship with a person from a different sector, different country, different religion – experience a real person, not just an idea, you've had eye contact – that is the first stage. Do I think craft, design and making can be a tool for social change? Yes, I do. They empower people to be part of a solution, not part of a problem. Sustainability on its own is not a good enough response; imagination without skills is not enough. Connectivity is part of the resilience we need.

Actual skills are the most valuable asset; the transferral of skills is essential to humanity. Surgeons fixing a shoulder use implants made with embroidery techniques. When I talk to makers, they have different attitudes to sharing knowledge. Blacksmiths are often very open – they used to be in the centre of the village talking to everyone. Whereas glassblowers and ceramicists are likely to be more secretive – one side of their heritage is about indoors and hidden discoveries, protected for luxury markets. For example, try asking a ceramicist about their glaze – no way they'll share the secret! We still need both sides – the amazing inventors who have the authorship, and also the openness to pollinate the ideas.

Ultimately this knowledge should be free and available, and the digital era allows us to share skills in a way we couldn't before. Videos capture the exact way people make things – every gesture, you can see it. You learn from people with experience, and how you apply those skills yourself to solve a problem is where imagination comes in. Computer screens no longer stop people from connecting. In fact, the digital has enabled us to learn again from other people, via forums, videos, webcams, live broadcasts.

One of the biggest problems we have is that there's a wall in perception: traditional crafts are not seen as part of our future. People look at 'heritage' as something that's happened – that's wrong. It's a continuum of knowledge. Put a 3D printer next to a dry-stone wall that's been around for ages – the way we learn about both is the same, from other people and from each other.

My interest is in the purposeful combination of traditional craft heritage with the contemporary and with the future. When people pick up materials, they're also making the connection between the knowledge that went into originally making the material and tools, their actual experience of manipulating the material towards a project, and the thought of how they can use that in future. Making is defeating that separation between past and future.

The Breadline collection by Bethany Williams
brings together the users of Trussell
Trust food bank in Vauxhall, south London,
supermarket chain Tesco, and a variety of
British craftspeople and artisans. Food-
bank users were invited to donate their
waste items in exchange for fresh fruit
and vegetables, which Williams combined
with waste materials from Tesco to create
the collection. Thirty per cent of profits
from sales of the clothing were donated back
to the Vauxhall food bank, continuing the
cycle of exchange.

Breadline
Bethany Williams

The Breadline garment collection by London designer Bethany Williams shows how corporate brands can connect with small-scale workshop activities and also with individuals in their locales. Breadline brings together an unusual set of collaborators: the Trussell Trust food bank in Vauxhall, south London, and its users, giant supermarket chain Tesco, and a variety of British craftspeople and artisans. The 'cycle of exchange' that Williams has set up uses design to respond to social and environmental issues, including poverty and recycling. How does it work? Tesco donates fresh fruit and vegetables and these are exchanged for waste items from the food-bank users' households. The Breadline collection is made from these waste materials, combined with recycled cardboard alongside other materials donated by Tesco. In turn, Breadline will donate 30% of its profits back to the food bank. Some of the most vulnerable members of the community thus both contribute to the project and benefit from it.

The garments themselves are all handmade and 100% sustainable, using techniques such as weaving, printing, knitting and embroidering. All components are either recycled or organic, and Williams has developed some innovative processes. For example, to turn her waste cardboard into usable fabric, she began by soaking it in water to separate its layers and fused these layers to organic cotton. This material was then laser-cut into forms that could be basket-woven. The resulting fabric feels like a soft leather.

Williams is particularly interested in the ways designers can provoke change within communities. She explains her own model: 'By using social capital, intellectual and labour-intensive skills we aim to create a profit, which will be given to connected charities, continuing the cycle of exchange. Through collaboration with communities and charities we hope to create a collection embedded with real people and hope to cause a real effect in the social space we engage with.'

Williams believes that fashion's relationship with a wide range of industries, from agriculture to communication, means fashion could become a force for positive change across a wide series of arenas. She applies her community minded principles not only in her work, but in her personal life: she is a regular volunteer for the Vauxhall food bank.

bethany-williams.com

The Granby Rock mantelpiece
is made of remoulded
demolition and construction
waste. Red and yellow brick,
slate and stone are cast with
sand, pigmented cement and
aggregate and then ground and
polished, creating a highly
decorative surface speckled
with rubble.

Granby Four Streets

Assemble

The Granby Four Streets initiative draws on design and making, founded in local heritage, to help rebuild a local community. Granby Four Streets in the racially and ethnically diverse Toxteth neighbourhood of Liverpool in the UK was for many years a rundown area full of boarded-up houses. Most of the streets here had been demolished, leaving the four that remained underpopulated and semi-derelict. Now it's a thriving community, following decades of hard work by local residents, who set up a community land ownership scheme in 2011 to begin converting empty homes into affordable housing. This work was supported by various partners, including the Assemble architecture collective, which reinvents problematic public spaces in cities, using design as a tool to improve social and cultural life. Granby Four Streets and Assemble won the Turner Prize for art in 2015; the judges praised 'a ground-up approach to regeneration, city planning and development in opposition to corporate gentrification'.

Granby Four Streets takes a distinctively people-centred, community-focused stance; Assemble members have described how they celebrate the idiosyncrasies of the derelict buildings. If a floor is missing, for example, rather than reinstating it, they might leave it out in favour of a double-height space. Because the project doesn't operate under the usual pressure to extract the maximum possible value from the site, it can put people before profit.

Assemble's Granby Workshop project is a social enterprise that trains and employs local people to make handmade products for the home. These items are made using experimental processes that invite improvisation: every one is different. The workshop's first range was composed of features designed for the refurbished homes in Granby Street, conceived to replace elements that had been stripped out of the boarded-up houses: mantelpieces were cast from brick and rubble construction waste, ceramic door handles were smoke-fired in barbecues, and tiles were decorated with colourful hand-cut decals, making a unique set of products perfectly in keeping with the community-led nature of the project.

Products now available to purchase online are diverse, from bookends and prints to lampshades and light pulls, all reflecting the talents and skills found locally. Granby Workshop also accepts commissions or can alter its existing designs for those seeking bespoke items, showing that a project on this scale is adaptable and nimble. Profits feed directly back into further development of the workshop. 'It is one part of a collection of projects that we have been working on to support the community-led regeneration of the area – exploring commercial structures that can also foster the creative, hands-on activity that has brought about such immense change in the area,' says Frances Edgerley, co-founder of Assemble. 'I think being embedded in specific locations and nurturing long-term, meaningful relationships with communities is important.'

Assemble's 18 members began working together in 2010. The collective's work practice is interdependent and collaborative; its philosophy is built around actively involving the public, both as participant and collaborator, in realizing its projects.

assemblestudio.co.uk

The Granby Workshop and showroom sells a range of products
that are made in Granby in one of the properties at
35 Cairns Street by a collective of local people using
experimental manufacturing processes. The first range
of products was a set of handmade features, designed for
refurbished homes in Granby to replace elements that were
stripped out of the houses as they were boarded up by
the council. These designs formed the first edition of
purchasable products, alongside new objects developed by
the Workshop team in collaboration with invited designers.

MATERIAL CONNECTIONS

All products are manufactured
using processes that embrace
chance, improvisation and
resourcefulness. Each product
purchased is unique. Profits
from their sale feed straight
back into the development
of Workshop, and will
also support a programme
engaging young people in the
area in creative and
practical projects.

FrankenToyMobile

Andrés Lemus-Spont, Marya Spont-Lemus, Louis Fernandez and Michael Pecirno

FrankenToyMobile brings together local communities in Chicago through crafting activities, as well as encouraging the repurposing of obsolete items.

The travelling studio operates from a custom-designed tricycle, and engages the youngest fledgling creatives – as well as adults. Toys that have outlived their original owners get a new lease of life here as they are repurposed into new creations: participants are invited to select old toy parts, decide what they want to make, and let their imagination take flight.

There are multiple community aspects to FrankenToy-Mobile. It is a mobile initiative that serves its local area in Chicago. The distinctive tricycle was deliberately chosen for its approachability; over the summer of 2016, it rocked up at parks, libraries, schools, exhibitions and other public spaces, often in underinvested neighbourhoods, actively seeking to spread its creative message as far as possible and lower barriers to access to arts workshops. FrankenToyMobile also hires teens and young adults whom the founders have taught or mentored, often from the communities the project serves, to help facilitate the workshops – for example, by teaching sewing skills or offering other technical support, as participants aged from four upwards cut, sew and glue to make their new creations.

'Our project is as much about bringing people together to share creative experiences and discover new talents as it is about the toys that are made,' say the founders – an interdisciplinary quartet of creatives whose skills encompass design, art, architecture and mechanics, and who set up FrankenToyMobile in June 2015. Creative interventions, they say, can bridge the boundaries that can prevent human connection.

This pedal-powered maker space sets out to democratize creativity and building skills, and encourage experimentation. It also helps young people challenge the concept of gendered toys. It relies on community engagement on various levels: from people who donate their old toys for repurposing; from volunteers who help facilitate workshops; from financial donors; and from those who invite the FrankenToyMobile tricycle into their communities and take part in the sessions with such enthusiasm.

frankentoymobile.com

Launched in 2015, FrankenToy-Mobile is a pedalpowered maker space that provides free hands-on workshops that invite children and adults to reuse and modify old toys, which turns public spaces into opportunities for community-based creative experiences.

By inviting young people to modify and re-engineer 'junk' toys, FrankenToyMobile encourages them to challenge dominant ideas about play and gendered toys. Workshop facilitators support the creative process as needed, teaching sewing and other fastening skills and serving as technical assistants to help make participants' visions reality.

Refugees Company for Crafts and Design
CUCULA

CUCULA (Refugees Company for Crafts and Design) in Berlin tackles the issue of integrating refugees into their new homes in Europe, helping them by enhancing their making skills and empowering them to build a new future. A combined workshop, education programme and meeting place, CUCULA welcomes refugees, gives them access to education and skills and, in the most practical way, gets them working on commercially viable design and craft projects.

The pilot workshop scheme began with six young West African men, all of whom had fled their homes and endured a difficult and dangerous journey to reach Berlin. CUCULA has established a lively workshop with a hands-on approach where refugees are building unique furniture and being trained in woodwork, construction and planning. At the same time, CUCULA Education offers academic classes, including language training, and legal advice, as well as social support, enhancing refugees' chances of obtaining an educational visa. CUCULA Education is financed through the sale of the furniture, alongside additional donations.

The 19 designs being made are taken from Italian modernist Enzo Mari's 1974 manual Autoprogettazione,

a pioneering work in the democratization of design; Mari's furniture collection can be assembled using basic materials and elementary tools. Mari has granted the CUCULA team the right to sell furniture based on his designs: 'a very good starting point to build a real business', as the team puts it.

The pieces available, made in pine wood, are all signed. They include the Sedia Uno chair, the Bambino chair for children, the Libreria shelves and the Letto bed. The crafters are also encouraged to incorporate personal artefacts into their work, to express both their history and their future.

CUCULA takes its name from the Hausa language spoken in West Africa and loosely translates as 'doing something together', as well as 'taking care of each other'. This collaborative model is based around working together and achieving together. It shows how the design community can take direct action to connect with global issues. CUCULA is striving for a 'pragmatic, immediate, action-oriented approach' – one that delivers concrete solutions.

cucula.org

Based in Berlin, CUCULA
(Refugees Company for
Crafts and Design) is an
association, a workshop and
an educational programme
designed to provide skills,
employment and a sense of
belonging for refugees.

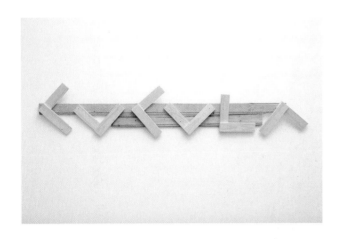

Trainees at CUCULA are taught
practical making skills, as
well as being given access to
other support networks such
as German-language classes
and legal advice. Based
on Enzo Mari's open-source
'Autoprogettazione' furniture
collection, the trainees
create high-quality furniture
pieces, proceeds from the
sale of which go directly
to fund their cost of
living and education.

The Bottle-Up project aims to tackle the issue of glass waste in Zanzibar. Caused by rapid increases in tourism, the country currently does not have the infrastructure to process or recycle the quantity of glass. Super Local travelled to Zanzibar to come up with design solutions to upcycle the glass waste. During the trip they worked together with local craftsmen to translate the techniques they used into a series of beautiful products.

Bottle-Up

Super Local in collaboration with Klaas Kuiken, OS△OOS and StoneCycling

The Super Local design studio uses design and making to find local solutions to local problems worldwide.

Luc van Hoeckel and Pim van Baarsen set up Super Local in 2015 to facilitate change and innovation that reward local populations through collaboration with local communities, practitioners and designers. The studio's founding principle is that solutions for social and cultural problems 'are always found in the country itself – by supporting the local economy, creating employment and encouraging entrepreneurship'. The studio, from its base in the Netherlands, works on projects that not only seek solutions to specific problems but also disseminate skills that provide long-lasting community benefit. The Bottle-Up initiative in Zanzibar is just one example. This tropical archipelago has become a popular tourist destination and, while holidaymakers are a welcome source of income, visitors also generate waste – including glass. As is the case in most of the destinations where Super Local works, there is as yet no way to reprocess or recycle waste, so the glass ends up being dumped.

Super Local sent a team of young Dutch designers to the country to explore ways to upcycle the obsolete glass, working with local craftsmen and, in a cleverly circular twist, making the waste glass that is thrown away by tourists into beautiful products those same tourists will buy and take home. The Bottle-Up collection includes storage jars, candle holders and decorative mobiles, all produced locally, by hand, and each one is unique.

The income generated not only supports local people and their skill development, but also provides funds to help solve the problem of the substantial proportion of waste glass that isn't suitable for repurposing into covetable souvenirs. The ultimate aim is to make this into construction materials for use across the islands; developments in progress include the bottle brick, made by combining glass and cement, and the Trending Terrazzo decorative material, a more refined mix of coloured glass shards set in white cement – its attractive shimmer makes it ideal for producing sustainable furniture, among other items.

The studio carries out extensive research to find out about each location, its people, and exactly what is needed. The approach is bottom-up, human-centred and collaborative. 'We want to make local communities proud and give them responsibility,' says Pim van Baarsen. 'We believe real sustainability is working with people and we want to make them part of the project.'

Collaborative projects such as these offer an immediate, tangible benefit in terms of tackling a specific issue – and the long-term benefits of sharing ideas and skills lend a lasting local momentum. As van Baarsen says: 'We eventually try to make ourselves superfluous. If that works, it means we did our job.'

super-local.com — bottle-up.org

Offering the Bottle-Up products to tourists
on the island completes the circle:
the waste caused by tourism is transformed
into beautiful, locally produced upcycled
products. The product line is just the
first step towards a cleaner island:
the income generated by the products will
be directly invested in the development of
more constructive solutions for processing
glass. The goal is to process large amounts
of glass waste into construction materials
that can be used on the island.

Beyond the Mainland

Phoebe Quare

Beyond the Mainland by Phoebe Quare uses modern design techniques to help a traditional region regain economic purpose.

The project asks whether a diminishing community and economy can be regenerated through reviving lost heritage using locally sourced materials. Bere Island is located off the coast of County Cork in southern Ireland. Its population, currently under 200, was over 2,000 at the time of the 1841 census; today, jobs in agriculture and fishing, such as mussel gathering, are supplemented by work in the tourism industry. Quare, whose MA from Central Saint Martins in London is in Material Futures, uses found materials from the island to produce artefacts that are locally significant and could help boost Bere's economy. Her creations include lamps made from a new material she has devised from mussel shells: the heated and ground shells, mixed with a natural binder, form a white plaster-like material. The design of the lights references the defensive Martello towers found on the island and military-style

signal lamps, drawing on Bere's military history. Quare has also gathered wool from the island's sheep to make woollen bags.

Designs such as these, she explains, could easily be reproduced and sold by local residents, opening up new revenue streams. The Material Futures MA course at Central Saint Martins blurs the boundaries between craft, science and technology in a trans-disciplinary approach that seeks to explore how we will live in the future. The approach of Quare's Beyond the Mainland is a mix of craft and tech-based knits, past, present and future.

mamaterialfutures.tumblr.com/Phoebe-Quare

Beyond the Mainland focuses on Bere Island, which is located off the coast of Ireland. The project aims to utilize local waste materials to create products rooted in local cultural traditions and practices and, in turn, provide new employment opportunities.

Quare reconsiders the resources of the island, using sheep's wool and crustaceans that would otherwise have been discarded. Developing a new plaster-like material made of mussel shells, she draws inspiration from the military heritage of the island to develop a collection of lights.

Sharing and pooling skills with the islanders, reinterpreting locally sourced materials, and drawing out traditions in the articles produced, the project aims to help economically sustain the population, enabling them to take more ownership of the island's future.

The People's Brick Company

Something & Son

The People's Brick Company by Something & Son delved, quite literally, into the brickbuilding heritage of London's Greenwich district, reinforcing the area's sense of place and belonging.

The bricks made on the Greenwich peninsula in the 19th century helped build one of the world's greatest cities: the People's Brick Company, a communal artwork, invited Londoners to bring this heritage industry back to life, and in the process make their personal mark on the neighbourhood.

The project was developed in partnership with the NOW Gallery, a permanent public exhibition space for contemporary art and design that opened on the Greenwich peninsula in 2014. The three-month process began in June 2016. People were invited to visit the People's Brick Company to make their own clay brick. Each brick, stamped with the maker's initials, was dried on a large rack in the gallery over the summer, in a constantly evolving display. The drying racks were made with waste timber from current construction works on the peninsula, and the wood was eventually burned to heat the kiln used to fire the bricks. The bricks were all fired during a public celebration in September and the end result was a permanent 'folly', or ornamental structure, conceived as a reminder that

architecture can be simple and inclusive. This interactive work was described by Jemima Burrill, a NOW Gallery curator, as 'a simple process which reflects on a larger state of being a part of a growing city.'

Something & Son's philosophy of collaboration has led founders Andrew Merritt and Paul Smyth to connect with professions as diverse as mushroom growers, scrapyard merchants, farmers, horticulturalists, scientists and sociologists. Of the People's Brick Company, they say: 'In a culture in which the production and origins of goods are becoming increasingly complex and exclusive, Something & Son is addressing a wish to return to the roots of our cities and in turn participate in the making of things.'

somethingandson.com

The Karawane collection reinterprets
the traditional Swiss craft of straw
plaiting. Hundreds of stems of wheat and
rye straw are plaited to make 'ribbons',
which are then sewn together. The plaited
straw work is made in collaboration with
straw-hatmaker Kurt Wismer from Switzerland,
one of the few artisans in Switzerland
who still practises the art.

MATERIAL CONNECTIONS

Karawane

Pour les Alpes

Zürich-based design studio Pour les Alpes develops relationships with traditional Swiss craftspeople and manufactories, reinterpreting ancient techniques into contemporary, high-quality designs to retain or revive heritage skills. Pour les Alpes, founded in 2014, is run by designers Annina Gähwiler and Tina Stieger, who met as students and graduated in industrial design in 2006.

The studio's Karawane collection reinterprets the traditional Swiss craft of straw plaiting, which has an unexpectedly oriental appearance but is rooted in Swiss culture. The straw-hat plaiting industry in Aargau, Switzerland, was one of the most important European straw trade centres of the 19th century. The Karawane collection includes a coffee table, a stool, a serving tray and a bowl. Notable for their organic shapes and combination of light, they are solid maple wood with delicate straw plaiting executed in wheat and rye straw. Hundreds of stems are plaited to make 'ribbons', which are then sewn together. The plaited straw work is

made in collaboration with straw-hatmaker Kurt Wismer from Hägglingen, Switzerland, one of the few artisans in Switzerland who still practises the art.

Gähwiler and Stieger travel through Switzerland seeking the traditional, unique and partly forgotten. 'We see ourselves as researchers,' they say. 'Inspired by traditional crafts and local myths, we strive to discover uniqueness. Creating products with a recognizable cultural identity is our main goal.' To this end, they work with artisans from across the country, including carpenters and lace makers, as well as master straw-plaiter Wismer. Of the straw technique, they recognize not only its particular Swiss characteristics, but its relationship with other artisanal skills from other nations: 'We are fascinated by the richness and complexity of this unique craft, which has many similarities with other techniques throughout the world.'

pourlesalpes.ch

5
Co-Creation

—

'Manufacturing is dead, long live manufacturing!' – We are on the cusp of a dramatic change in the way that we make things, a shake-up that promises to alter fundamentally the way we live and work, potentially rebalancing our relationship with our planet and reshaping society for the better.

Communications and computing have already experienced transformative disruptions. Now it is the turn of manufacturing to undergo a similarly dramatic upheaval, enabled by technology and in particular the democratization of digital fabrication tools. Although we do not yet know how the effects will unfold, the changes we face are so profound that the talk is of a fourth Industrial Revolution. After the first industrial revolution adopted water and steam power for manufacturing, the second harnessed electric power for mass production, the third applied information technology to automate processes, now the fourth iteration of an Industrial Revolution is characterized by a fusion of emergent technologies that blur divisions between the physical, digital and biological worlds.

One thing is beyond doubt: the old model that relied on turning a supply of rapidly dwindling raw materials into products shipped around the world to be discarded when obsolete now appears hopelessly past its sell-by date. In a world in which billions of people are connected via mobile devices with unprecedented processing power, storage capacity and access to knowledge, the idea of manufacturing being centralized, wasteful, expensive and exclusive is as outdated as fax machines and the abacus.

Emerging technologies, including artificial intelligence, robotics and nanotechnology, are already filtering down from the laboratory to the industrial world, but some of the greatest strides are being made in the field of digital fabrication tools, where an exponential increase in the pace of technological change coupled with price decreases is bringing manufacturing to the masses. Democratization of digital fabrication is paving the way for an atomized and distributed network of makers. Already, small, highly specialized manufacturers are springing up all over the world, offering downloadable designs, pre- and post-purchase customization, and production on demand. This new manufacturing flexibility has started to transform our economy and the relationship between the producer and the people.

Powerful, lower-price industry-grade 3D printers, CNC routers and laser-cutters are enabling people to design, model and engineer their creations themselves locally. In private workshops, at home and in maker spaces, hack spaces and Fab Labs, these new technologies are disrupting top-down business models by transforming the way we make and distribute goods. Digital fabrication promises a waste-free, more sustainable, less expensive, more co-operative and holistic system of consumption. For decades our moribund retail cycle has gambled its fortunes and our planet's resources on wasteful presumptions of what the public wants. More often than not, large quantities of products are left unsold, un-needed and unwanted.

Recent advances in open-source and digital design as well as networked technologies are now paving the way for decentralized production and post-purchase manufacture that promises to put an end to dull, uninspired over-production of goods. In the field of <u>Downloadable Design</u>, products are only manufactured when they have a home in which they really are needed and wanted. Designing for digitally enabled production allows designs to be kept 'soft' for longer, so faults can be corrected with less waste which makes the idea of ultimate <u>Digital Bespoke</u> more feasible. Cutting-edge manufacturing technologies promise more sustainable, less wasteful production processes. Additive manufacture, which is becoming increasingly refined and applicable to a wider range of materials, avoids raw material production waste and enables <u>Crafted Mass Production</u>.

1

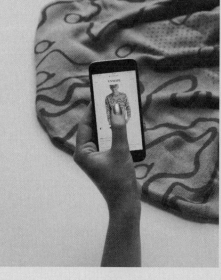

2

3

4

5

6

Digital Bespoke

Bespoke pieces, such as couture fashion and commissioned artworks, have traditionally been the preserve of the super-rich. At the other end of the scale, mass-produced, cookie-cutter products lack cachet and desirability. Mass customization bridges the gap. By hacking the back end of the production process, decision-making over details is handed to the people and customization is performed early in the manufacturing process, rather than tacked on at the end.

1 — Convivial Project by Ann-Kristin Abel and Paul Ferragut
2 — Unmade

Downloadable Design

Excess production is a major headache for manufacturers and alienates the waste-averse among us. Downloadable design and post-purchase production is about needs and wants – exactly what's needed is made exactly when and where it's wanted. The design is downloaded at the point of purchase, customized to the customer's requirements and made locally. No waste. No redundancy. No compromise.

3 — Opendesk
4 — The Post-Couture Collective by Martijn van Strien

Crafted Mass Production

In the digital age, designers and makers are looking to blend the digital seamlessly with the tactile to combine the efficiency, autonomy and productivity of digital fabrication with the emotional resonance of crafted imperfection.

5 — Functional 3D Printed Ceramics by Olivier van Herpt
6 — L'Artisan Électronique by Unfold

Joni Steiner

Joni Steiner is co-founder
and creative director of
Opendesk, an open-source
furniture company that
distributes the manufacturing
of furniture through a network
of independent local makers.
He is also a qualified
architect and founding member
of the strategic design studio
00 and open-source housing
platform WikiHouse.

We didn't set out to start a company. We were just playing around
with technology and digital fabrication and realized that when you
have the right digital design tools you can question the 20th-century
model of manufacturing because you can distribute both the
processes of manufacturing – the design and the making. Therefore,
you can create much more local, human-scaled social supply chains.

Of course, when you start to build the thing, you realize there are
hurdles. A table might only specify a shape of a leg and a shape
of a top, and you can play with the size and shape of both, but when
you interface with the nuts and bolts of making things, you realize
there are constraints. So, although we are super-excited about
co-creation, we have had to deliberately constrain ourselves. For us,
replacing the traditional factory with a network of independent
makers is in itself the challenge. We've focused on the relationship
between a set of designs by designers who understand and believe
in sharing, and a network of makers who believe in using digital
fabrication with simple materials such as plywood and new,
recycled sheet materials that are starting to come through.

Attitudes are changing. We've seen it in food; people will now buy
an imperfect apple because it has the right narrative, because

a particular farmer who didn't use unwanted chemicals grew it. The value is clear and it's less about any superficial imperfections, which could be seen as virtues as long as the customer understands why. I think we're living in a moment when longer-term benefits of purchase or design decisions are becoming very current.

We're really excited by the idea that customers should have an alternative to mass production that benefits the producer. We communicate material costs, but also the amount the maker gets paid as a percentage. And part of the story is that your piece is being made specifically for you. I think nearly everyone thinks that's a good thing. Obviously you have to ensure consistency of appearance and quality, but people value the craft of the individual maker's hand after the machine has done the cutting work.

What excites us about CNC technology is that it's not new at all. Its maturity brings increased access through lowered costs, alongside latent skills and capacity around the world. There are downloadable plans to make fully functioning CNC machines in your own garage using bought-in electronic and cutting parts and then milling your own parts to improve the machine so that it becomes higher resolution. A company called Shaper is bringing out a CNC targeted at the home market like a high-end power tool. It's got a screen where you upload a design that you trace on the screen, so it's basically a CNC router but doesn't involve a massive amount of machinery around it. With Kickstarter and other platforms, there is a great movement towards democratizing such tools.

Something such as Shaper won't be able to compete with an industrial machine, but we think some Opendesk makers will be using Shaper by the end of 2017. It's an exciting time and it opens up the possibility of manufacturing at smaller scales, maybe incorporating co-design and co-creation, reintroducing small-scale, niche manufacturing into urban areas and revitalizing industries through plugging into a technology as a tool to empower humans rather than to replace humans.

We believe that technology should serve us, not the other way round. What's important for us is technology that's about bringing people more and more into the story of making.

The pattern of each Convivial
scarf can be manipulated
using an algorithm to ensure
each design is unique to
each customer.

Convivial Project

Ann-Kristin Abel and Paul Ferragut

Founded by Ann-Kristin Abel and Paul Ferragut in 2014, Convivial Project is a London-based experimental design studio that has developed a website and an iPad/iPhone app to put the creative process of designing clothing into the hands of the customer.

Having graduated from Central Saint Martins, London, Ferragut, a graphic designer and creative technologist, and Abel, a fashion designer and researcher, decided to combine their skills and experience to explore their passion for innovation in design and to craft bespoke goods and wearable pieces using emerging technologies.

Aiming not just to sell their creations, but also to empower people to generate designs themselves, they created a web application and an iOS app that enables customers to become co-creators. Generative Scarves, the duo's debut collection, involved using the web application or iPhone app to generate abstract patterns based on mathematical algorithms. These patterns can be digitally printed onto silk scarves (and, subsequently, leggings) finished in the UK.

Although the concept of mathematically generated patterns might sound highly technical and possibly over-complicated for customers, the duo made it as easy in practice as pushing a few sliders on a screen to tweak colours and adjust pattern parameters such as fluidity, intricacy, frequency and scale.

The project, which Ferragut says 'began as a creative coding experiment', resulted in unpredictable and intricate visual landscapes of melting shapes and colours that have been described as 'mesmerizing patterns giving an illusion of movement unusual in a traditional print'.

Giving customers increasing autonomy and control over the look of their products is an 'interesting step', says Ferragut, in the evolving relationship dynamic between creators and consumers that is bridging the gap between the maker and the user. 'We believe that especially small companies who are more flexible and more keen on taking risks to drive innovation will propose customization,' he adds.

Customers can choose the material (silk or wool), specify the fabric's qualities (soft sheen or matt silk) and select from two algorithms titled Fractional Motion and Vertices. Fractional Motion is based on a procedural algorithm known as Perlin Noise, commonly used to generate patterns of the natural world. 'The results,' says Convivial Project, 'are individual and striking, representative of the elemental characteristics of liquid metals, minerals and organic formations found in rocks, presented through an infinite choice of stunning colours and textures.'

Vertices, the studio's second algorithm, is based on a three-dimensional mesh of polygons, edges and faces defining landscapes and surfaces. 'By altering the moving elements, you affect the formations produced,' says Convivial Project. 'The dimensional textures, grids, and movements are akin to fabrics blowing in the wind, forms of rugged landscapes, oceans and many more.'

Pre-designed scarves cost £170 on the design studio's website. Customer-designed 120 x 120 cm (47 x 47 in.) scarves cost £220 and delivery takes up to three weeks. Ferragut concedes that 'of course prices won't be the same as mass-produced items in foreign factories, but we would achieve a higher-quality product and crafted value instead of quantity.'

convivialproject.com

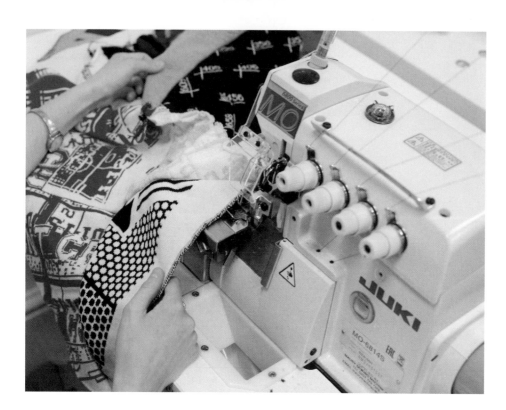

Left:

Unmade knitwear is
adapted and customized
digitally by the customer
before being knitted by
a hacked industrial knit
machine and skilfully
joined by hand.

Below:

The interactive interface
allows users to shift and
scale surface patterns.

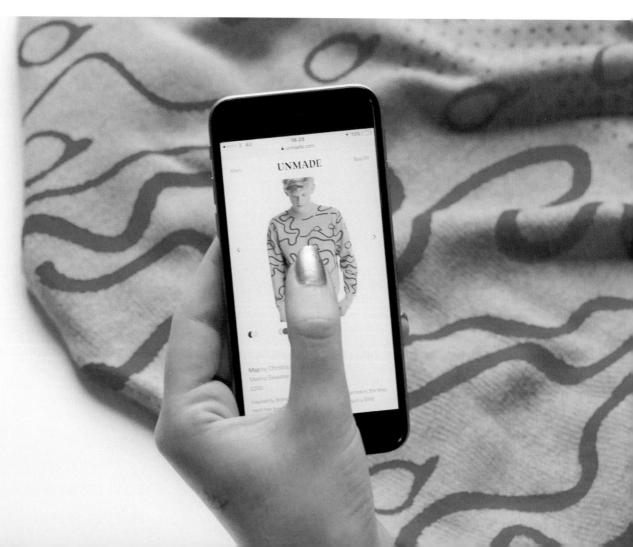

Unmade

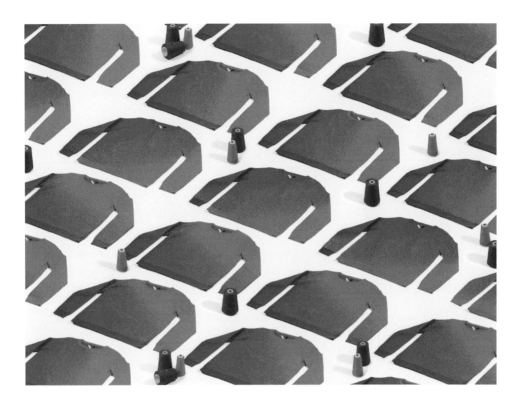

Described by the Daily Telegraph as 'the future of knitwear' and by the New York Times as 'out to change the fashion industry, one knit at a time', Unmade is a London start-up that enables customers to design their own luxury sweaters and scarves made at Unmade's own on-demand knitwear factory (apparently the world's first). They are delivered within five days, all via a cloud platform and website.

In fashion, where lead times are usually specified in months, Unmade's disruptive technology was created in response to its founders' frustration at the industry's lethargic attitudes to mass consumption. Ben Alun-Jones, creative director and one of Unmade's three founders, describes the start-up's mission as 'putting an end to made for everyone, designed for no one' and 'creating bespoke for the modern era'.

While researching performance clothing for UK Sport, Alun-Jones and his partners, Hal Watts and Kirsty Emery, realized the untapped potential of industrial knitting machines. Combining their programming and engineering skills, they developed a new way to control them. 'Everything is unmade,' says Alun-Jones, 'until the customer chooses their design, when industrial machines whirr into action and knit a one-of-a-kind item for a similar cost to mass production.'

At present, customers aren't given an entirely free hand in their designs: they are led through a 'curated customization' process in which knitwear developed in collaboration with designers such as Christopher Ræburn and Kate Moross can be tweaked – or 'unmade' – by the customer, who sees their creative contribution acknowledged in their name stitched into the label.

Describing clothes 'as a series of parameters', Alun-Jones says: 'We control some of them and Christopher has controlled some of them, and we've left some open for the customer to control.' Among the parameters open to customers is the ability to choose colour combinations, to move, zoom or break apart the pattern or to insert their initials into the design. In one example, the garment is made from a customer's favourite location on a stylized version of a map of Borneo created by Ræburn. In time, Unmade hopes to allow customers a much freer hand in the design process than the current disruptive approach.

Having worked on projects with the British Fashion Council, designed an award-winning catwalk collection with Ræburn, built a concept store within Selfridges and popped-up a store in Covent Garden, Unmade set up its knitwear factory in the Makerversity incubation space at Somerset House Studios in central London.

As well as creating a new way to overcome supply chain, design and retail limitations, Unmade's three element system – personalization editor, e-commerce integration and on-demand manufacturing – also promises less waste. Currently, a tenth of manufactured clothing never sees a shop, heading straight to landfill because it's deemed unfit for purpose. Less waste means savings for both customer and producer.

unmade.com

Opendesk

With the potential to disrupt the furniture industry in the same way Airbnb has disrupted the hotel business, Opendesk offers furniture designs that can be downloaded from its website and be made anywhere in the world. This cuts out the middle-man supplier and reduces waste, transport and storage costs.

Inspired by an observation by economist John Maynard Keynes that 'it is easier to ship recipes than cakes and biscuits', Opendesk is an adherent of a new manufacturing model – Open Making – which makes designs from all over the world easily accessible so that they can be produced locally. 'At the moment, one has to make a choice between entirely bespoke products and mass-produced products typically made where the land and labour are cheapest, then shipped large distances,' says Nick Ierodiaconou, Opendesk's head of product and one of its five founders. 'Instead of us owning factories and doing manufacturing, or owning shops and holding stock of products, through the Open Making model everything gets manufactured on demand as local to the customer as possible.'

The Open Making process is strikingly simple. Designers submit work and choose licence terms specified for commercial and non-commercial use. Customers choose to download the digital design file to DIY-build items themselves in a maker space, or work with a trusted local fabricator from Opendesk's global network. Like 3D-printing and laser-cutting, CNC milling is a digital manufacturing technology. It uses a computer-controlled drill to cut parts from sheet materials such as plywood, Smile Plastics and Solidwool – a composite made from bio resin and waste wool.

At present, Opendesk has more than 30 product designs on its website, ranging from desks, tables and chairs to bookshelves, lockers and pedestals. It works with approximately 400 fabricators in 32 countries. However, Open Making's most disruptive impact isn't the technology so much as the social process that it unlocks – the experience of engaging in the way something is made, close to home and customized precisely to purpose.

Kickstarted by a furniture commission for the New York office of a London tech start-up (designs were sent to a local manufacturer rather than shipping the completed product), Opendesk now predominantly supplies workplace furniture to creative companies and non-profit organizations. Clients include Google, Nike and Greenpeace, who kitted out their London Islington HQ with Opendesk desks, tables and storage made just a few miles away in the centre of Hackney.

Such clients are typically drawn to a combination of the flexibility of the designs, the speed of delivery and of course the local fabrication story – Greenpeace actually specified that they wanted to visit the workshop by cycling over in their lunch breaks, and the Open Making model made this possible! On top of this, clients have a keen eye for a good deal that doesn't compromise the producer. According to co-founder Tim Carrigan, 'around 8% of an Opendesk goes to the designer, which compares favourably with the 3-5% designers would usually receive on a mass-production model, and the maker takes about 70%, rather than 20–30%.'

Furniture making is one part of a growing Open Making movement. Architects and Opendesk co-founders Joni Steiner and Nick Ierodiaconou, together with colleague Alastair Parvin, were also behind a sister project called WikiHouse. The same principle is applied to architecture – with the tantalizing promise that in the future we might be downloading not only our furniture, but also the homes in which to put it.

opendesk.cc

The library of designs covers
workplace-focused furniture
from chairs, tables and desks
to lockers and room dividers.

Garments from The Post-
Couture Collective engage
with a post-purchase
production model. They can
either be shipped, pre-cut
and ready for stitch-free
joining, or alternatively
delivered as a digital file
so that the purchaser can
produce the garment from
scratch in their chosen
fabric.

This page:

Modular Chiffon Dress, part
of The Antwerp collection.

Opposite:

The Post-Couture Collective
launch collection.

Overleaf, left page:

Wool wrap skirt from
The Post-Couture Antwerp
Collection.

Overleaf, right page:

Customers are able to choose
to buy designs digitally.
They are given instructions
on how to cut and assemble
the garment pieces.

The Post-Couture Collective
Martijn van Strien

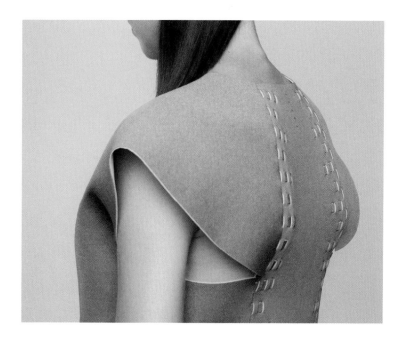

Claiming to be the first brand to combine the maker movement with the third Industrial Revolution (aka the digitization of manufacturing), The Post-Couture Collective is an open-source project that lets customers design their own clothing to be manufactured locally on laser-cutters and 3D printers.

Founded by Martijn van Strien, a graduate in textile design and trend forecasting from the Design Academy Eindhoven, it comes laden with green credentials, such as an end to the rampant waste that plagues the fashion trade, as well as much of the transport of garments. Van Strien says that because Post-Couture garments are 'designed on the spot by our software' and 'produced only when they're sold' his approach avoids creating the obsolete 40% of garments that arrive at shops only to be discarded at the end of each season.

One Off, his first collection, comprises six pieces, all costing less than £100 and all personalized to a customer's measurements. Designs are then either downloaded to be cut locally on a laser-cutter or shipped to the customer as a kit. In both cases, the garments feature seams that slot together, eliminating the need for sewing.

'Offering people a chance to influence and be part of the design and production process of their garments will create much more attractive products than the current mass-manufacturing industry does,' says Van Strien. 'Who wouldn't choose a garment that is designed and made especially for them and their body shape over something standard that everybody else has?'

In keeping with maker culture, Van Strien's methods democratize production so that all garments can be 'produced anywhere by anyone', he says. 'All of the normal construction techniques are eliminated, so no sewing, no seams, no training.

We're introducing a new way of thinking about sustainability, embracing the maker's movement and cutting out unfair labour, overproduction and waste in doing so.'

Spacer fabric, a soft, breathable and malleable 3D-knitted material similar to neoprene, is specified for all the garments, although Van Strien is entirely happy for customers to select appropriate local materials, hoping that choice of material and customization options would help to give his garments 'a lot of added emotional value'.

'I have nothing against beautiful clothes or looking good,' Van Strien adds, 'as long as we enjoy it consciously and without the damaging effects on people and the environment. Currently materials are grown in very specific parts of the planet. They get transported to the few countries that produce most of our clothing and then the garments are spread around the world again. Trying to have all those aspects – material, production and consumption – in the same location could have a huge impact on the carbon footprint of this industry.'

Van Strien's preference for a synthetic fabric flies in the face of the usual demand for natural, preferably organic, materials but in fact creates a more sustainable closed-loop system. Recyclable a second time after wearing, Spacer is made from recycled PET bottles that determine the fabric's colour – green, grey-white or grey-black – depending on the hue of the plastic.

postcouture.cc

Lasercutting

You've choosen your fabric and found a lasercutter nearby that you can use. That's all we need!

So...
Let's make it!

TIP place your fabric in the lasercutter with the darker side facing up → this way it will make up the best cuts.

Material suggestion
This garment was designed to be made from a thin polyester fabric.

Our Orange and Black-and-White versions are sourced from Belgium.

Components

The XL-SLeeve Blouse consists of 28 strings and 7 components that need to be lasercut.

TIP to save fabric (and time) you can make pairs or place more components next to each other. For example component ②③ or ⑤⑥.

Cutting sheet (A)
min. fabric sheet width: 250 mm
min. fabric sheet height: 150 mm

Cutting sheet (B)
min. fabric sheet width: 500 mm
min. fabric sheet height: 600 mm

Cutting sheet (C)
min. fabric sheet width: 1100 mm
min. fabric sheet height: 650 mm

Cutting sheet (D)(E)
min. fabric sheet width: 1050 mm
min. fabric sheet height: 700 mm

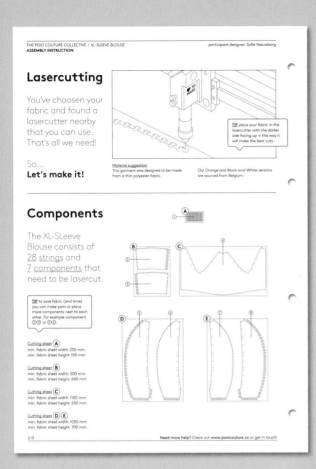

Connectors

The XL-Sleeve Blouse is equipped with connectors and slots.

Assembly System
A connector ⓒ has to go through a slot ⓢ. The connector can connect to another component or it it can connect itself.

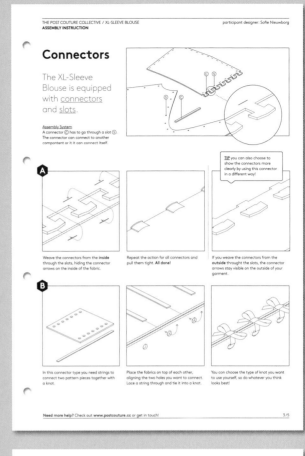

TIP you can also choose to show the connectors more clearly by using this connector in a different way!

A Weave the connectors from the **inside** through the slots, hiding the connector arrows on the inside of the fabric.

Repeat the action for all connectors and pull them tight. **All done!**

If you weave the connectors from the **outside** throught the slots, the connector arrows stay visible on the outside of your garment.

B In this connector type you need strings to connect two pattern pieces together with a knot.

Place the fabrics on top of each other, aligning the two holes you want to connect. Lace a string through and tie it into a knot.

You can choose the type of knot you want to use yourself, so do whatever you think looks best!

Assembly

Now that we know how the connectors work, we can start assembling.

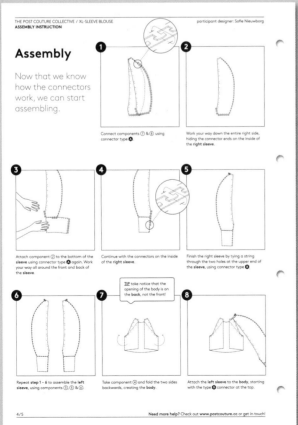

1 Connect components ⑦ & ⑤ using connector type **A**.

2 Work your way down the entire right side, hiding the connector ends on the inside of the **right sleeve**.

3 Attach component ② to the bottom of the **sleeve** using connector type **A** again. Work your way all around the front and back of the **sleeve**.

4 Continue with the connectors on the inside of the **right sleeve**.

5 Finish the right **sleeve** by tying a string through the two holes at the upper end of the **sleeve**, using connector type **B**.

6 Repeat **step 1 - 6** to assemble the **left sleeve**, using components ①, ③ & ⑥.

TIP take notice that the opening of the body is on the **back**, not the front!

7 Take component ④ and fold the two sides backwards, creating the **body**.

8 Attach the **left sleeve** to the **body**, starting with the type **B** connector at the top.

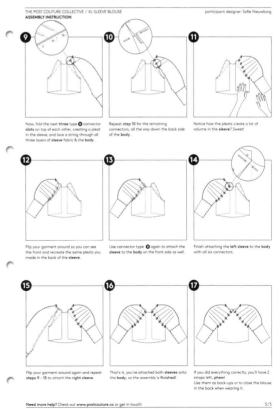

9 Now, fold the next **three** type **B** connector **slots** on top of each other, creating a pleat in the sleeve, and lace a string through all three layers of **sleeve** fabric & the **body**.

10 Repeat **step 10** for the remaining connectors, all the way down the back side of the **body**.

11 Notice how the pleats create a lot of volume in the **sleeve**! Sweet!

12 Flip your garment around so you can see the front and recreate the same pleats you made in the back of the **sleeve**.

13 Use connector type **B** again to attach the **sleeve** to the **body** on the front side as well.

14 Finish attaching the **left sleeve** to the **body** with all six connectors.

15 Flip your garment around again and repeat **steps 9 - 15** to attach the **right sleeve**.

16 That's it, you've attached both **sleeves** onto the **body**, so the assembly is **finished!**

17 If you did everything correctly, you'll have 2 straps left, **phew!**
Use them as back-ups or to close the blouse in the back when wearing it.

Van Herpt's clay extruder
enables the creation of
intricate 3D clay structures
with surface textures that
would not be possible
by hand.

Functional 3D Printed Ceramics

Olivier van Herpt

Olivier van Herpt, an industrial design graduate of the Design Academy Eindhoven, has taken clay coil ceramics, one of mankind's oldest handcrafts, and reinvented them for the digital age. Over two years at the academy, van Herpt developed his own 3D clay printer in response to his frustrations with the technical and artistic capabilities of existing 3D printers and 3D printing materials.

'The desktop 3D printers on offer were unable to produce things at a human scale,' he says. 'Large- and medium-scale functional design objects that we use, such as bowls, plates and decorative objects, could not be made. The objects made with desktop 3D printers were also low in heat resistance and could not be food safe.'

Although industrial 3D printers were capable of making food-safe objects for everyday use, the printers were very large and the finished items were too costly to produce. Van Herpt's response was to design and make his own clay extruder, which led him to create a range of visually stunning, intricately knitted ceramics with a scale and level of detail that would be nigh on impossible using traditional artisanal methods.

His breakthrough came as a result of a long process of iterative experimentation and improving his process that gradually solved major issues such as the collapse of objects. Forcing clay through the nozzle of conventional 3D printers required the clay to be softened with water, but objects larger than 40 cm (16 in.) collapsed under their own weight because of the softness of the clay. Van Herpt decided to abandon mixing clay with water and use industrial strength motors to deposit a thicker paste of ordinary potters' clay.

'By redesigning my extruder I could use hard clay instead. This led me to be able to make larger items with higher levels of detail,' he says. 'In the early days, the 3D printed ceramic vases and bowls seemed rough, with the layers clearly visible.' But after experimenting with textures, surfaces, shapes and sizes, he was eventually 'able to make objects up to 80 cm (31 in.) tall with a diameter of 42 cm (16½ in.). By altering the settings on my machine I can vary and give the pieces very different appearances.'

With textures reminiscent of fine lace or natural forms, the finished products appear handcrafted, but their intricacy reminds the viewer that they are a collaboration between man and machine. 'Clay is a much more elegant and noble material than plastic, it is much more sculptural,' says van Herpt, who has exhibited his functional ceramic objects in two collections, the 3D Woven Collection and the Sediment Collection.

'3D printing has the potential to bring back the unique and individualized objects that artisans make,' the designer says. 'But this time it is a machine who manufactures the final product. Each unique vase in this collection shows us the potential of cutting-edge technology while reminding us of the days of yore.' He adds that the Sediment Collection has some of the thinnest 3D-printed ceramics layers possible today. 'The fine stria remind us that the object was 3D printed but only when one is close to it. The physics, materials and 3D printing challenges shape these objects. In guiding and exploring the forms I enjoy playing with geometric shapes that are not perfect geometries, and making things that would be difficult or impossible to make with other processes.'

Van Herpt's subsequent project, Solid Vibrations, came about after he noticed subtle changes in the clay as a result of vibrations from sound and, once again, began experimenting. Working with sound designer Ricky van Broekhoven, he developed a system in which a speaker emits a low-pitched drone directly beneath the printer as it slowly pipes the vessel. Vibrations from the speaker create moiré patterns in the clay that look very much like textile knits and act as visual representations of sound made permanent.

oliviervanherpt.com

CO-CREATION

The designer believes that
rather than replacing
craft, technology can aid
the preservation of craft
practices.

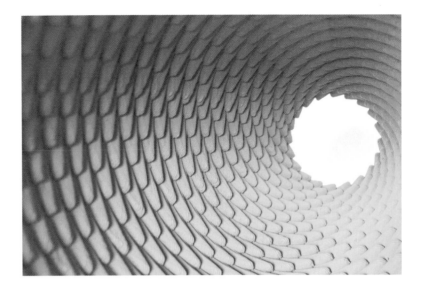

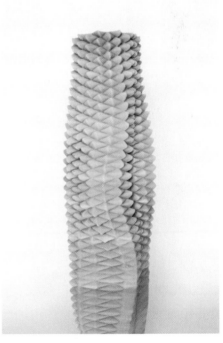

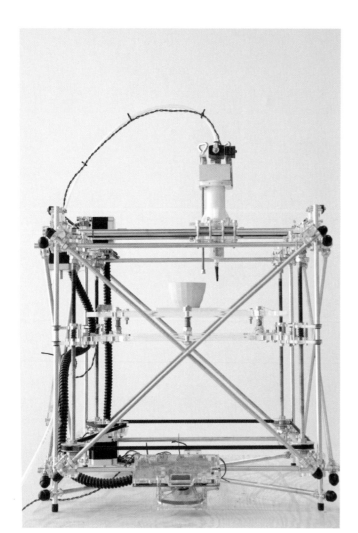

L'Artisan Électronique is a digital ceramic
tool described as a virtual pottery
wheel. Users can hand-shape the wire-frame model
of a clay vessel in mid-air by simply
tilting and moving their hands within
the field of a connected digital scanner.
The digital design can then be 3D printed
at a local Fab Lab or print shop.

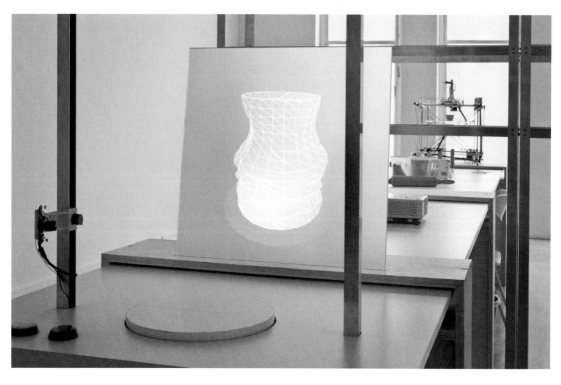

L'Artisan Électronique

Unfold

Unfold is an Antwerp design studio that explores the possibilities and potential realities of personal fabrication technology and its impact on modes of production and traditional crafts.

At the heart of Unfold's exploration is the open-source RepRap 3D printer developed in 2005 by a small group of students led by Professor Adrian Bowyer at the University of Bath. RepRap (the Replicating Rapid Prototyper), is a low-cost 3D printer that can print most of its own components and thereby replicate itself. When the blueprints were published online, a community of makers, inventors, designers, artists and hobbyists joined in its development, improving and extending its capabilities and sharing their discoveries in a 'blog of blogs' that catalogued RepRap's rapid evolution.

Among those empowered by RepRap's lowering of the barriers into digital manufacturing was Unfold, founded in 2002 by Design Academy Eindhoven graduates Claire Warnier and Dries Verbruggen to develop projects that investigate new ways of creating, manufacturing, financing and distributing products. 'We think it is important that designers again get a connection with their tools and learn how to use them,' says Verbruggen. 'Instead of contracting out the work, sending someone a digital file and receiving a finished product, we want to design the tool ourselves and understand it again. Our research has always focused on the 3D printing of ceramics because plastic seems nice, but to most people it looks cheap and disposable. The opposites of this are ceramics and porcelain.'

One of Unfold's earliest projects in which they modified a RepRap with a special tool head for printing clay was called Stratigraphic Manufactury. It involved taking the machine to Istanbul to investigate how local craftspeople adapted their own skills on the 3D printed products, adjusting thicknesses of layers and using local clays and glazes in a process that Verbruggen describes as half craft and half robot. It was, he says, 'an exploration of how there can be a lot of difference in manufacturing through a distributed network.'

More recently, Unfold developed another ceramic-making tool: l'Artisan Électronique. Described as a virtual pottery wheel, it allows exhibition visitors to hand-shape the wire-frame model of a clay vessel in mid-air by tilting and moving their hand within the field of a 3D scanner controlled by digital design software. Verbruggen says this could allow people to create ceramic objects online and then print them out at their nearest 3D printing shop or Fab Lab, in what he describes as 'a virtual networked factory'.

This, he adds, is how Unfold sees design in the future: 'when personal manufacturing is more ubiquitous the designer will have to let go of some control over the final design. Customization has to be more playful than just choosing the colours of your new sneakers.'

unfold.be

F-abric by Freitag.

6
Designed to Disappear
—

Approached in the right way, disposable consumables could help to solve waste issues instead of adding to them. Innovative designers suggest that rather than encouraging abstinence from consumption, a sustainable future may be found in throwaway products made from materials that disappear.

Sustainability has previously focused on reducing consumption, but the growing acknowledgment that the hunger for 'new' is far from satiated is causing a shift in the way that designers conceive high-volume, low-cost items. Innovations include designs with built-in easy end-of-life recycling and products created to serve a function, then harmlessly disappear.

Our insatiable appetites for cheap items, fast fashion and fast-moving consumer goods contribute greatly to landfill. A large percentage of the textiles made into apparel is never sold and actually ends up as waste. Research shows that 288 million tons of plastics is produced worldwide each year; around a third of the world's plastic is used to make packaging that is mostly discarded after use. This excess waste has become a global concern: France has become the first nation to initiate a ban on all plastic cups, plates and cutlery. The ban, which comes into effect in 2020, is part of the government's plan to promote a circular-economy waste-disposal system; only items made of compostable materials will be exempt.

However, as retailers well know, consumers have an infinite appetite for the new, the exciting, and the up-to-the-minute, and this is unlikely to change any time soon. There are other factors at play here too: consumer desire for convenience frequently outweighs environmentally related concerns. Designers are tackling the challenge head on. Longevity will always be a desirable quality in some fields, but in industries such as fashion and packaging, currently characterized by high-volume production, low retail prices and little recycling, as well as an imperative for low prices, there is a new embrace of what could be characterized as the temporary. These goods do the job equally adeptly as their conventional counterparts, but are subsequently straightforward to repurpose or simply to make disappear.

Environmentally aware designers are taking responsibility for the afterlife of their creations even while those creations are still on the drawing board. They are also seeking to tread lightly or not at all in terms of environmental footprint. In a closed-loop or circular economy – the most desirable model for sustainability – materials that came from nature go back to nature, or the product is remade after at the end of its useful life.

Designers and material innovators are using different tactics to achieve functional closed-loop models even in industries long characterized by wasteful single-use production. Short Life materials and products, seen principally in packaging that lasts only as long as its contents or that is biodegradable or even edible, serve their purpose and then vanish. Designed for Recycling, which focuses on reuse at the time of product conception, deliberately chooses materials that are straightforward to recycle and can be placed into existing recycling infrastructure. And concern over the long life of synthetics such as oil-based plastics are leading designers to seek Zero Legacy by developing alternative media, both mono-materials and composites, that biodegrade naturally and harmlessly.

1

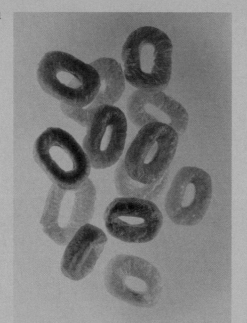

2

3

4

5

6

7

Short Life

Mass-produced consumer goods and discarded packaging are major pollutants and contributors to landfill. Designers are addressing this by developing both packaging and products that acknowledge the insatiable human appetite for consumption, yet disappear entirely after use.

1 — Agar Plasticity by AMAM
2 — EcoGrill by Lou Moria

Designed for Recycling

Creatives in various disciplines are making repurposing a cornerstone of their initial designs rather than an afterthought, whether they are working with entirely new materials or focusing on materials that can fit into existing recycling systems.

3 — Short Life by Kay Politowicz and Sandy MacLennan
4 — Polyspolia by Will Yates-Johnson

Zero Legacy

Synthetic materials such as oil-based plastics can take centuries to break down; some never vanish at all. Eco-conscious designers and brands are seeking to develop viable biodegradable substitutes in fields as diverse as fashion and furniture, drawing on the transitory qualities of biodegradable mono-materials, composites and bioplastics.

5 — Collection 1 by Crafting Plastics! Studio
6 — Flax Chair by Christien Meindertsma
7 — F-abric by Freitag

Kate Goldsworthy

Kate Goldsworthy is reader
in circular textile design
at the University of the Arts
London, and a lead researcher
with the university's Textile
Futures Research Centre. She
collaborates with science
and industry partners on
sustainable design projects.
Her work has been focused on
designing out textile waste
and understanding environmental
impact since 1998.

Fantastic leaps are being made in material recovery. It's now possible to take textile waste and turn it into virgin-quality fibre. The science is getting very close – we're talking five to 10 years rather than the distant future. Most of the focus is on recycling polyester and cotton, and those two are around 40% of the market each, so if you can crack those, you are well on the way. The block to scaling is going to be supply: getting the materials back from the consumer in quantity, with a regular flow. However, most of our clothing currently goes out to Africa for reuse and new legislation is going to stop that, so we're going to be in possession of more waste clothing. Large companies such as H&M are investing in this tech: they are well aware that there will be supply problems with virgin materials in the future. We're working with two European multi-partner consortiums on fibre-to-fibre recycling.

The other interesting development in terms of scaling is not top-down change by big companies, but bottom-up, grassroots systems. Several companies have set up online clothing reseller market places that take out all the hassle for the consumer. Systems that encourage the consumer to put unwanted clothing back into the system are going to be massive.

You can't easily change people's behaviour, but you can give them better options, either by making positive action very easy for them, or by devising an invisible system they may not even be aware of. The system needs to be either something that people love, or something that works efficiently in the background.

We are looking at the slow and fast in the fashion sphere to try and understand the impacts and also find the positives and bust some myths. There's an assumption that slow is best and fast is bad, but we have both fast and slow cycles in nature and they work together in harmony. If we could do both better, perhaps by thinking about fast as multiple small cycles and about slow as one extended cycle, they could be equally positive. Recycling over and over again might be just as good as having an item that you keep for longer, but that is very heavy in its production footprint. And if the solar and renewable energy problem is solved in the future, and we have unlimited energy, that will change everything.

Designers have so much responsibility and power, yet it's very difficult for them to access information so they can understand potential impact even before they get their materials – or understand how their design decisions affect the story. Recovery needs to be built into every design brief. Younger designers especially are very aware of this.

Small companies have an interesting role. They are flexible, and many actions across a big group can have a big impact. They can also act as pioneers for the big companies – and there is a real desire for change in the big companies, although they are slower to move.

There has to be a synergy, a symbiosis across industries, which is a real challenge. For example, textile fibres can be made from food industry waste, but just connecting those two industries is quite a big leap. There are various examples: polyesters from methane, the use of orange fibre, waste milk. As well as cleaning up our own industry through fibre-to-fibre technology, we can also help clean up other industries' waste. And we even have the potential to clean up existing materials. Some polyesters contain chemicals that are now banned; during recycling, we can take these out. We can use regenerative technology to help undo past mistakes.

Agar Plasticity
AMAM

Agar Plasticity, an ongoing material research project by Japanese design trio Kosuke Araki, Noriaki Maetani and Akira Muraoka of the AMAM studio in Tokyo, was picked from over 1,200 entries to take the Lexus Design Award Grand Prix at Milan Design Week 2016. The project explores how agar, a gelatinous material extracted from marine algae, can be used as an environmentally friendly packaging material.

Cushioned in agar-based material, a fragile bottle posted in Japan arrived in Milan intact – a successful proof of concept for a project that involved lengthy research.

Millions of tons of plastic are produced across the world each year, around a third of which is used for packaging. Much of this ends up in landfill or polluting the ocean, and many plastics biodegrade very slowly – some over centuries. This is the problem that Agar Plasticity sets out to tackle.

Already well-known as a culinary ingredient, particularly in Japan, agar has various scientific and medical uses. It is extracted through boiling red algae, a seaweed harvested across the world.

Using pure powdered agar, AMAM produced a package with integrated cushioning and a thin, transparent film, loose-fill cushioning similar to the familiar polystyrene 'packing peanuts'. The designers also experimented with combining agar powder and red algae waste fibres that are currently used only as fertilizer. Combining these waste fibres with algae powder

produces a harder, thicker composite material that can be used as wrapping for flowers, cushioned-packaging of fragile materials or moulded to make boxes.

AMAM has also looked into the potential of combining agar powder with shell 'ash', a by-product of the food industry. Mixed with water and agar, shell 'ash' becomes mouldable and tough; the AMAM designers suggest it could even be used to make building materials such as wall tiles. All three variations can be disposed of in an environmentally friendly manner. Buried in soil, they not only act as a fertilizer but also improve water retention because agar absorbs and holds moisture. If they end up in the sea, they biodegrade harmlessly.

With packaging essential for all types of industry, an alternative to plastic that performs its job well then breaks down swiftly and even beneficially would find myriad uses. The designers are currently seeking industry partners to further develop their research. They believe algae-based material could replace plastics in other areas beyond packaging, such as shopping bags, cable ties, toothbrushes, ballpoint pens, even cutlery.

a-ma-m.com

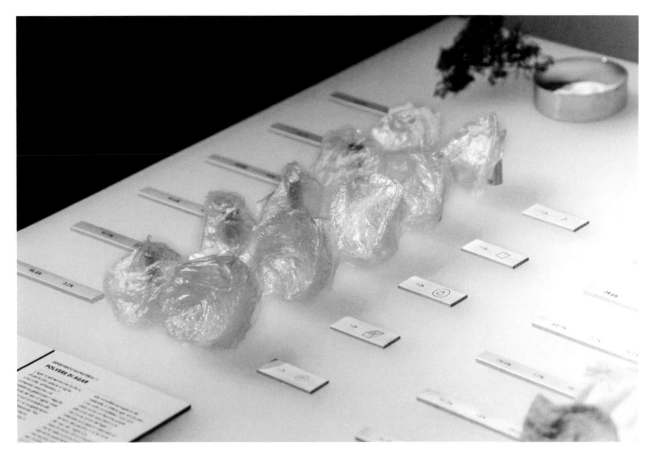

Top:

AMAM created a biodegradable algae-based material as a proposed substitute for conventional plastic packaging.

Above and right:

The material that is procured by boiling red algae, a common seaweed found in Japan, could also be used to create a biodegradable replacement for synthetic polystyrene 'peanuts'. The material that is derived from the ocean will ultimately end its life dissolving harmlessly back into it.

Opposite:

AMAM looked into the potential of combining agar powder with shell 'ash', a by-product of the food industry.

Below:

As the exterior material burns it slowly cooks the food inside, leaving behind nothing but ash and a compostable clay plate.

Opposite:

The EcoGrill is a single-use outdoor oven woven out of pine and paulownia tree fibres.

EcoGrill

Lou Moria

Israeli designer Lou Moria's EcoGrill takes the notion of short-life disposability to the limit by offering an item that is destroyed by fulfilling its function.

Designed for exterior use and knitted from fibres of the pine and paulownia trees, the EcoGrill looks a little like a beehive resting on a clay plate base. Food is popped into the woven chamber, which is tied closed before the grill is lit. The interior pine fibres are coated with a natural combustion agent to ensure the grill catches light easily, unlike conventional barbecues, which can prove problematic for the cook. The whole thing smells deliciously of the forest as the food inside slowly cooks.

By the time the woven exterior has burned away, the food is ready. The remains of the EcoGrill, including the clay plate, can be left to decompose into the Earth, with no need for any further recycling.

This biodegradable slow cooker offers a new way of thinking about food and food preparation, says the designer. The project prioritizes a very clear ecological approach. All components and materials are 100% organic and return to the Earth during the cooking process. The concept was influenced by cradle-to-cradle waste-free design principles that reflect the lack of waste in the cycles of the natural world.

As well as the practicalities, the EcoGrill also exhibits a cultural aspiration that reflects the principles of the Slow Food movement. The cooking process, says Moria, 'creates an event – an excursion out into nature, the slow cooking process, the preparation, the cooperative aspect involved in preparing the food. All these are values the Slow Food movement is based on.'

The knitted design was developed because it facilitated control of the burn process, says the designer, adding that each fibre functions as a wick that kindles other parts of the weave. Pine and paulownia burn for the necessary time to complete the cooking process and in combination emit an appetizing fragrance. Different spices can be woven into the wood fibres to enhance the scent and taste of the meal.

loumoria.com

This page:

A non-woven fabric made out of plant-based lyocell is used in the collection that is intended for single or limited wear before disposal.

Opposite:

The collection of men's and women's garments is proposed as a way to tackle the issues of fast fashion.

Short Life
Kay Politowicz and Sandy MacLennan

Kay Politowicz, co-founder of Textiles Environment Design at Chelsea College of Arts, explores strategies for sustainable design innovation and product improvement to develop interconnected design thinking for new products.

In collaboration with designer Sandy MacLennan, Kay Politowicz is producing a range of Short Life garments based on material developed in the paper industries. Faced by a rapidly expanding fast-fashion culture, Politowicz and MacLennan are seeking to fulfil consumer desire for endless novelty in a way that is environmentally friendly and sustainable. Their Short Life garments are designed for single or very limited use before disposal – with the added benefit of eliminating laundering, which also has an environmental impact of its own.

Short-life addresses increasing raw material shortages by using material that can be recovered over and over in a recycling loop. The non-woven fabric, made of plant-based lyocell, is stronger than paper but has similar attributes, thereby dramatically increasing the environmental credentials of short-life garments while simultaneously offering huge potential for creating aesthetically desirable clothes.

Helping to facilitate a cooperative approach to sustainability, the collection brings together the previously unrelated fashion fabrics, paper manufacturing and recycling industries in this proposed closed-loop system of production, disposal and regeneration. Other businesses could also get involved; the development of a new aesthetically attractive and practical non-woven clothing product might attract companies that are working on cellulosic fibres designed to replace cotton (a thirsty crop that requires global transport).

Using substrates and processes normally associated with other industrial applications is a way to keep costs low while producing in very high volumes. An engineered short-life textile can thereby satisfy the desire for consumption followed by disposal, but at the same time set up a virtuous circle of renewal. By recognizing and accommodating throwaway culture it also alleviates consumer guilt. In other words, if you can't beat them, join them.

tfrc.org.uk

Polyspolia
Will Yates-Johnson

Will Yates-Johnson's Polyspolia project takes inspiration from Willy Wonka's Everlasting Gobstopper, a sweet that not only changes colours and textures, but can never be finished and never gets smaller. The attractive, tactile pieces, which include lamps, clocks and pots, are as brightly coloured as the gobstopper itself.

The designer's starting point for the collection's concept was to give each item a potentially infinite afterlife; each object can be endlessly broken up and remade. Yates-Johnson quite literally takes his father's old mallet and smashes up existing pieces to make new ones.

Yates-Johnson, a graduate of the Royal College of Art, London, says his work 'occupies a space between art and science'. Interested in rethinking systems and production processes, for Polyspolia he trialled many thermosetting plastics, including polyurethane and polyester resins – natural successors to Bakelite's phenolic resin.

Various fillers of different grades were also tested, from sawdust and wood flour to calcium carbonate, aluminium hydroxide and talcum powder. The final material's composition means it can be broken into fragments and reformed into new products over and over again; all old material is incorporated into the new iterations, and not a crumb is wasted. Furthermore, Polyspolia uses a chemical process that requires no external energy to create new products – and this also sidesteps thermosetting plastics' resistance to melting, a clever solution to one of the material's limitations.

Derived from the Greek for many (poly) and the Latin for spoils (spolia), Polyspolia's name also references spolia, the ancient Roman custom of reusing earlier building parts to create new constructions with no attempt to hide the 'recycling' element. Polyspolia pieces are similarly open about their recycled origins; the fragments of the older pieces can clearly be seen, and Yates-Johnson uses contrasting colours for each Polyspolia 'generation' to give a visual demonstration of the recycling process. Most products, observes the designer, are disposed of once they reach the end of their useful lives or fall out of favour. 'Polyspolia proposes instead a new kind of relationship to material resources that makes visible the process of recycling, transforming and enhancing in beauty and complexity each generation of products,' he says. 'The project offers an alternative to consumer society's expectations of newness based on the fantasy of infinite resources.'

whyj.uk

Polyspolia is a proposed
cyclical manufacturing
system. Once a product has
outlived its usefulness or
desire it can be broken up
into fragments and recast
into a new item.

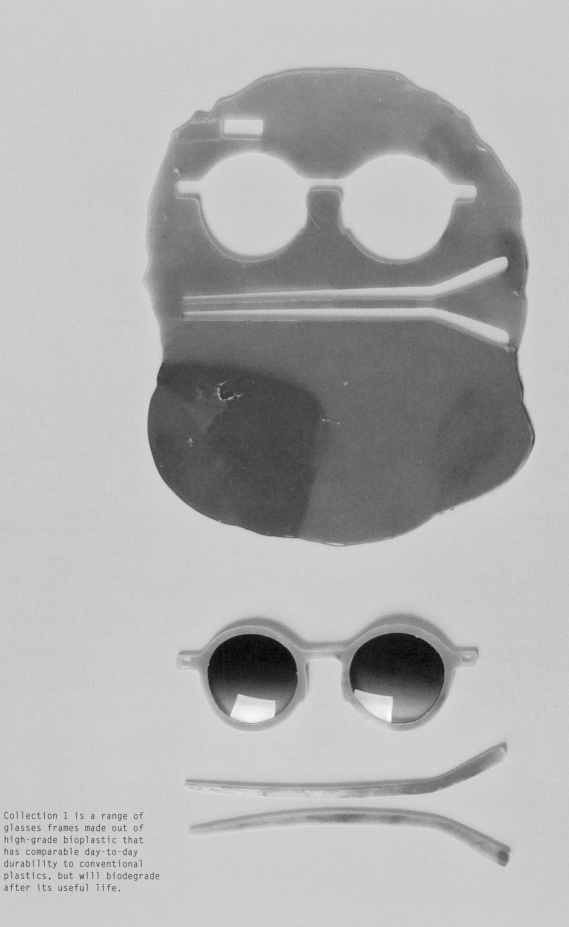

Collection 1 is a range of
glasses frames made out of
high-grade bioplastic that
has comparable day-to-day
durability to conventional
plastics, but will biodegrade
after its useful life.

Collection 1
Crafting Plastics! Studio

'We make perishableness valuable,' says the team at Crafting Plastics, a Berlin studio that works with bioplastics derived from plant material.

Product designer Vlasta Kubušová and fashion designer Verena Michels, the duo behind the studio, experiment, collaborate and produce with a product's whole lifecycle in mind, using techniques that range from craft-based to those requiring high-tech machinery. The aim is to keep full control of each product's lifespan, from its origin as unrefined material, through its useful life, until it finally decays, thus taking responsibility not only for the design and function that any designer would consider, but also for decommissioning or disposal.

The studio's first product, a collection of sunglasses, straightforwardly named Collection 1, was launched at Spazio Rossana Orlandi during Milan Design Week in 2016. When the glasses are finished with, they can be industrially composted or composted in the garden heap or returned to the company for composting or recycling.

Crafting Plastics developed its own bioplastic with specialists at the Slovak University of Technology in Bratislava. Compared to other bioplastics, it performs extremely well in daily use and the company is working on new processing methods specifically geared to bioplastics, often considered

lower grade than conventional plastics. For instance, they melt several layers together to improve durability, or they fuse the plastic with textile fibres for extra strength.

'The seemingly lower-grade properties of bioplastics actually enable us to process them using original crafting methods. The unique visuality – new to bioplastics – is a direct result of this process,' say Kubušová and Michels, who have experimented with raincoats as well as the Collection 1 glasses frames. 'Each frame is an evidence of engaged research in bioplastics and technology: material and technology translate directly into design.'

Kubušová and Michels seek to bring useful products to market and inspire producers to carry out further research into bioplastics. Their ultimate aim is to revolutionize the conventional perception of consumption by making perishability precious.

craftingplastics.com

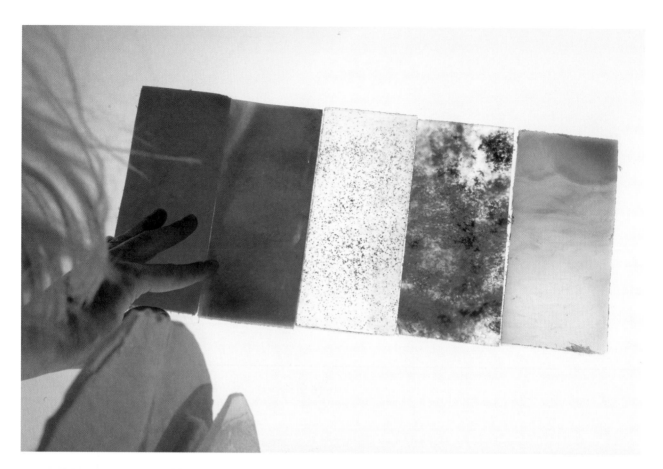

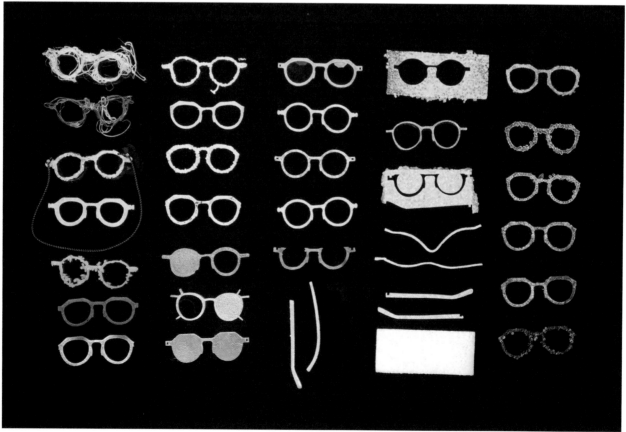

DESIGNED TO DISAPPEAR

When the glasses are
finished with, they can be
industrially or domestically
composted, or returned to the
company for recycling.

The Flax Chair is made
of a composite of flax
fibres combined with PLA,
a biodegradable polylactic
acid derived from sugar cane
or corn starch. Consequently,
the piece is made of entirely
renewable materials and is
totally biodegradable.

Flax Chair
Christien Meindertsma

Dutch artist and designer Christien Meindertsma has said that today's designers should not be thinking in terms of designing the antiques of the future; rather, their products should fit into a circular system and be designed according to the material that goes into the product, but also what it leaves behind after use. After all, even items created to last will eventually become obsolete, and designers need to predict that redundancy and plan for it. Her Flax Chair is a perfect example of this philosophy. It was created for Label/Breed, an initiative that matches designers with manufacturers. Meindertsma worked closely on the project with Enkev, a global enterprise based in the Netherlands that makes environmentally friendly, high-quality filling and covering materials from natural fibres.

Both woven and felted flax are used to make the chair, which when heat-pressed with the bioplastic emerges as a strong, solid material. The simple, attractively shaped chair is constructed from a single sheet – a single panel for the seat with the remainder of the sheet folded to make the legs, thereby minimizing waste. The natural materials generate a neutrally coloured item, but the composite can be dyed, so a rainbow-hued range of flax furniture is a future possibility.

One of the attractions of using flax, says the designer, is that it is a hardy plant that grows well across the world. She also likes its historic association with high-quality fabric such as linen, and has experimented with various other uses for this versatile plant.

Taking a material more commonly used for fabric and rope and developing a solid chair with strength, comfort and good looks was a technical challenge, but, in collaboration with Enkev, Meindertsma rose to it, so successfully that Label/Breed has taken it into production. A winner of two 2016 Dutch Design Awards, the chair has been purchased by the Vitra Design Museum.

christienmeindertsma.com

 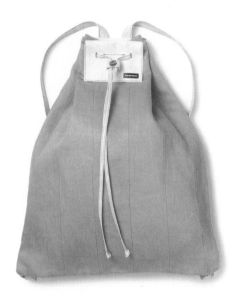 

Above:

F-abric workwear is designed to last and last, but once the pieces are done with they will rot away, leaving nothing behind.

Opposite:

F-abric is made from bast fibres – strong, cellulosic fibres obtained from plants: in this case, European-grown hemp and linen. These are combined with Modal, a semi-synthetic fibre derived from beech wood.

F-abric

Freitag

'Do textiles really have to be shipped across the world three times over before they reach us?' pondered Daniel and Markus Freitag, the brothers who founded well-known and much-loved Swiss brand Freitag. The answer, it turned out, was 'no'. Not only is there no need to transport textiles around the globe before they are made into garments, but there is also no need to ship them away for disposal.

The Freitag brothers began their business over 20 years ago, making their famous signature messenger bags from used truck tarpaulins. They have now come up with F-abric, an entirely biodegradable textile produced in Europe. At the end of its useful life, F-abric clothing breaks down 100% naturally, including garments' threads and selvage (prototypes sewn with polyester thread composted within months, other than the thread, so it was back to the drawing board to find a more environmentally friendly alternative).

No bleach is used during production, the number of chemicals used is minimized and dyes are low-impact. All of the production stages take place within a 2,500-kilometre radius of the company's Zürich factory.

If the idea of hempen clothing conjures up images of shapeless hippie-style attire, be reassured, although the company admits that the 'challenge is to process these fibres into a fabric that continues to impress'. The F-abric range, which includes men's and women's lines of shirts, trousers, T-shirts and rugged five-pocket jeans made with no rivets or polyester threads, retains all the original cool Freitag style.

These are clothes that will last and last, but once they are done with, they will rot into the ground. 'A piece of clothing thus becomes fertile soil for new raw materials and the cycle continues,' says Freitag, which refers to its products as 'prêt-à-composter'.

The final challenge that still eludes Freitag is to come up with a satisfactory biodegradable trouser button. But this can only be a matter of time...and meanwhile, the tough, reusable buttons that currently feature in the collection can be unscrewed, removed from the garment, and repurposed.

freitag.ch

Fruiting mycelium material,
part of The Future of Plastic
by Officina Corpuscoli,
Maurizio Montalti.

7
Living Materials

—

We are beginning to use the by-products of living systems as materials for design. The quest for sustainability and an ecological approach for design models is leading us towards a scenario where biological manufacture replaces industrial manufacture and living entities are engineered to grow materials and products. Designers and material innovators are mimicking the closed-loop, circular systems found in the natural world to enable the production of biodegradable materials from fungi and bacteria.

Environmentally conscious designers are rethinking basic building materials. Engaging with our resource-threatened future, they are using biomimicry and engineered nature to find sustainable alternatives to synthetic materials such as oil-based plastics. High-tech advances in material technology are paving the way for a closed-loop and zero-legacy future. New composites, produced by living creatures and designed to degrade entirely or to fit into a circular economy, are the novel building blocks of sustainable design.

Held in Paris in 2013, the 'Alive' exhibition curated by Carole Collet, professor of design for sustainable futures at Central Saint Martins, London, suggested that we 'imagine a world where biological fabrication replaces traditional manufacture, plants grow products, and bacteria are genetically reprogrammed to "biofacture" new materials, artefacts, energy or medicine.' In the few years since the exhibition was held, the leap of imagination required to bridge the gap between concept and reality has shrunk.

Suzanne Lee, founder of BioCouture, a pioneer of producing fabric and clothing from bacteria-generated cellulose, refers to microbes as 'the factories of the future'. She is not the only forward-thinking designer challenging our perceptions of natural materials by growing fabric and other items from bacteria, yeast, fungi and algae. Designers, architects and material engineers are collaborating with nature to develop new techniques to grow and craft consumer goods, products and packaging.

Techniques range from the ancient to the very modern. Tropism, where external stimuli such as light and nutrient regulation influence plant growth, has been known for centuries. Cellular agriculture, the derivation of agricultural products from cell cultures (such as making plant-based products that are molecularly identical to meat) is very much a 21st-century phenomenon. In this sphere, man's attempts to control nature could be seen as positive rather than negative – perhaps more akin to cooperation than exploitation. Sensitive manipulation of biomimicry could prove the route to a more sustainable future relationship with our planet.

As Maurizio Montalti of the Officina Corpuscoli design studio in Amsterdam points out: 'One of the main challenges of the current century is to transform our consumption-oriented economic system into an eco-friendly and self-sustaining society, capable of minimizing energy consumption, carbon emissions and the production of waste, while reducing production costs.' Designers are addressing the sustainability challenge by working from the ground up, creating new materials from basic cellular building blocks. Growing acceptance of biotechnology and synthetic biology is leading to laboratories that begin to resemble farms. Cellular agriculture in particular is gaining ground and is increasingly believed to be a viable future sustainable food resource. Why take from nature when you can grow an exact – or improved – replica without causing any harm?

The Power of Fungus is a particularly promising avenue. Fungi grow at a rapid rate and their underground mycelium (their equivalent to a plant's roots) find multiple uses. Form, size, texture and surface quality can be easily manipulated and mushrooms feed happily on agricultural waste, making this a low-cost, non-polluting, entirely biodegradable material option.

Designers who espouse the Grow Your Own principle are creating DIY systems to enable anyone and everyone to recycle their waste and create their own products. Others are taking a slower-paced approach: Engineering Growth turns plants into living factories that are simultaneously the material, the design and the end product.

1

2

3

4

5

6

7

8

The Power of Fungus

Mycelium, derived from fungi, is gaining a reputation as a new wonder material. Easy-to-cultivate and fast-growing, it can be manipulated to adopt the properties of many mainstream materials, including leather, wood, stone and polystyrene.

1 — MycoWorks
2 — The Growing Lab by Officina Corpuscoli
3 — From Earth: Mycelium Textiles by Carole Collet

Grow Your Own

Bacterial by-products are proving to be cost-effective, environmentally friendly media with wide-ranging applications, prompting designers to develop processes and equipment to enable biological production at home.

4 — Growduce by Guillian Graves and Aakriti Jain
5 — The Grow It Yourself by Krown Design
6 — Invisible Resources by Zuzana Gombosova

Engineering Growth

Systems that impose a degree of control over nature, such as tropism (using factors such as nutrient and light supply to influence plant growth) could be used in the slow cultivation and manufacture of materials – and even whole products.

7 — Botanical Craft by Carole Collet
8 — Interwoven by Diana Scherer

Maurizio Montalti

Maurizio Montalti is the founder of design and research practice Officina Corpuscoli, which focuses on developing the practical uses of mycelium. He is also a partner in MycoPlast, a collective project working on viable alternatives to synthetic materials.

Everybody has a role to play in making positive change: individuals, policy makers, industries, and so on. The role of the designer is central. I believe designers have a great responsibility. They act as catalysers of change. Design as a language allows the transmission of complex information in an accessible form. While designers can develop new perspectives, it is also fundamental that they take the next step for action, going beyond experimentation – a step that goes further than demonstrating feasibility, and towards implementing promising innovations.

We are already in the middle of a transition. My hope, from what I see around me, looking at the work of other practitioners, is that many new materials will replace the traditional standards, such as those based on fossil fuels. We're looking here at a large range of materials derived from living processes: materials grown using cells, crops that can be processed to create other compounds. There might be quite a drastic change in the next 20 years, but in the next decade a lot will already be happening: research is being developed into real applications that will come to market.

Biofabrication and engineered nature offer a very large spectrum of possibilities. The potential for amazing scientific tools such as synthetic biology are infinite; we may even create alternatives that out-perform traditional fossil-based synthetics. This introduces another big topic: how we use such tools and the ethical questions they raise. This is the most exciting conversation. In order to create this change, to speed the transition, it's fundamental to create a cultural shift and encourage critical thinking.

Micro-organisms such as fungi are often associated with disgust, looked on as pathogens. In fact, very few are harmful. Designers have to explain the benefits of a symbiotic relationship between humans and these different life forms. Sensorial experience must be incorporated into the work: I have found it paramount, when exhibiting, that people are allowed to touch the materials, smell them, move them around.

Living materials are a little more unpredictable than traditional static matter. My company is concerned with stabilizing and scaling-up products and that's a great challenge. To conform to industry standards, products need to be repeatable, have consistent qualities, be formed in the same amount of time, and have the same technical characteristics. But the fact that these materials are living is an advantage – and we need to question this attitude that everything has to be perfected, which is fundamentally unnatural. We need to re-evaluate the subject of imperfection. To work with mycelium, you kill the fungus: it becomes inert. Working with material that keeps living, in a state of perpetual transformation, is currently adopted as part of the more artistically-driven practices. But one day it may be possible to grow objects for the consumer market with specific qualities and in desired shapes, starting from the very information contained in the DNA of the living materials/partners.

The function of the creative practice, art or design, is to open doors where nobody sees an opening, to create new forms that nobody would expect. I envisage a future factory as clearly ordered, similar to factories today – but much more alive. My sketches of the future factory are like fields of cultivation, with both micro and macro entities – fungi, algae, crops…however, such factories will not be there for growing food, but for growing semi-finished and finished components. I have no crystal ball – but I think, in general, the best way to predict the future is to invent the future!

MycoWorks

MycoWorks in San Francisco produces a mycelium-based material with all the properties of leather, but without a cow in sight – a win-win scenario for humans and bovines alike.

MycoWorks has found that Ganoderma lucidum, a mushroom used in natural remedies in Asia for centuries, is particularly versatile. Cultivated on readily available agricultural and industrial waste such as sawdust, corn husks, paper pulp and hemp cores, the resulting material is strong, flexible and durable. Like leather, it is water-resistant and breathable. It also feels just like conventional leather, which helps overcome the 'yuck factor' sometimes associated with fungus-based materials.

Fungi-derived leather even has advantages over the traditional product. MycoWorks can grow fastenings, textures and patterns into the material. Using simple tropisms, it encourages the fungi to grow in specific ways by controlling nutrient availability and environmental factors such as temperature, humidity and light levels. Unlike animal hide, it can be grown to fit any size or shape and can be produced in a fraction of the time it takes to raise a cow, with far less resource input.

The production process is carbon-negative. Importantly, it is a closed loop that uses abundant natural resources to create an entirely biodegradable material, making an infinitely renewable technology that points the way towards mono-material circular production.

Co-founder and chief technology officer Philip Ross, an artist, inventor, entrepreneur and visiting scholar at Stanford University, points out that we will never run out of the resources necessary to produce mycelium-based material. 'Mushrooms work through decomposition,' he says. 'There is continual generation of organic matter; we can guarantee it. We can look at that and call it garbage, but it is a resource that can provide for us. It is potentially your food, your house, even your jacket.'

The MycoWorks team, which aims to 'build a better world with nature's best tools', combines creative engineers, designers and scientists. It draws on more than 20 years of research into designing and engineering mycelium materials.

'Making mushroom-generated materials is not so very different from growing food, and the processes we use, such as pasteurization, are globally distributed. People grow crops all over the planet, people grow mushrooms all over the planet,' says Ross. 'You hear a lot about ideas that might happen in 10 years' time but this stuff is here, it can grow now.'

mycoworks.com

This page:

MycoWorks materials
in a range of finishes,
from natural textures
to dyed and patterned.

Opposite:

Co-founder Sophia
Wang in MycoWorks's
San Francisco
production studio.

Left:

Mycelium Bowl with fungi, part of 'The Future of Plastic', an ongoing research project looking at the potential of replacing our habit of plastic production with 'Growing Design'.

Below:

Fruiting mycelium schyzo.

The Growing Lab

Officina Corpuscoli

The Growing Lab at Officina Corpuscoli, a design practice based in Amsterdam, is an ongoing research project that explores the practical application of mycelium in developing new materials and processes.

Founder Maurizio Montalti's approach is creative and transdisciplinary, bringing together creativity with research-based, experimental techniques and drawing on themes related to biotechnology, anthropology, production technology and other disciplines.

The Growing Lab poses the question 'What is the potential of high-(bio)tech, craft-based thinking, when combined with open-source, made-to-measure processes?' and is pursuing various research directions in search of the answer.

With a particular focus on seeking substitutes for synthetic oil-based plastics, the project ultimately considers a shift from traditional industrial production methods to one that is based in cultivation – going from a 'making factory' to a self-sustaining 'growing factory'. Items produced so far include attractively irregular and rugged bowls, pots and vessels, and 'textiles', all created using minimal energy and generating minimal CO_2 and waste.

Montalti is also a partner in MycoPlast, a collective project that aims to provide a sustainable, viable alternative to synthetic materials derived from fossil fuels. MycoPlast

is developing MOGU, an industrially viable way to use mycelium-derived materials at scale. Following the principles of the circular economy, it is targeting its light, low-density, strong, shock-absorbing functional materials at industries such as construction, packaging and horticulture. The initiative works with 3D designers, 3D printing and modelling engineers, biologists, biotechnologists and business development managers, again reflecting Montalti's multidisciplinary approach.

Officina Corpuscoli was commissioned to create a project for 'The Future of Plastic', a 2014 exhibition commissioned by Fondazione PLART, a Naples-based foundation that focuses on research into design and art in plastic. The project outlined a practical vision of how plastic materials could come to life, and brought the studio's work on 'cultivated objects' derived from fungus to a wide audience.

corpuscoli.com

Top:

Pure mycelium flexible textile sample, part of The Growing Lab's ongoing experimentation into the potential of grown materials.

Above:

Pure mycelium samples, part of 'The Future of Plastic'.

Opposite, above:

'The Future of Plastic', a 2014 exhibition showcasing the studio's research into the potential of 'cultivated objects' derived from fungus as an alternative to plastic products.

Opposite, below:

Mycelium vessels.

LIVING MATERIALS

Left:

Sample showcasing a permanent fold resulting from the moulding technique.

Below:

Mycelium is fed waste coffee grounds as it grows on vintage and paper lace.

Opposite:

Self-patterned mycelium rubber; the floral fractal patterns are not the result of any kind of moulding process, but instead they slowly grow on the surface of the material as it develops over a period of three weeks.

From Earth: Mycelium Textiles

Carole Collet

The Design and Living Systems Lab at Central Saint Martins, London, is a research laboratory that explores the interface between biological sciences and design, with a particular focus on envisioning sustainable materials and forms of production. The lab is directed by Carole Collet, professor of design for sustainable futures, who has centred her career around developing new visions for design and is particularly interested in biodesign, biofacturing and sustainability.

From Earth: Mycelium Textiles, one of the lab's varied projects, explores the potential of mycelium grown as a sustainable new surface treatment for textiles. The project aims to produce both soft and structural textile qualities by manipulating the environment in which the mycelium is grown; to develop biodegradable, compostable textile coatings to replace finishing processes derived from oil; and to encourage self-patterning techniques in mycelium materials, which is a new field.

The various mycelium are cultured on a variety of materials that either harness, support or resist the fungi's growth; these include coffee grounds, agar, hemp, sisal, soya-bean fibre, raw silk, organic cotton and linen. Developments include a mycelium lace, where the living material serves to reinforce and mend the lace it grows on and a self-patterned mycelium 'rubber'. The latter is as flexible as rubber, and exhibits 'floral' patterns that are not created by moulding, but by the mycelium itself as it grows on waste coffee substrate. This is the first known example of a self-patterning mycelium material. 'The "flowers" you see in the sample grew on the surface of the material by themselves,' says Collet. 'I grow the mycelium in a sealed, clean environment, then bake it to kill the material, so it's inactive. After the baking, I brushed off the coffee grounds and was surprised to find the "flowers".' While this project is still at an early, experimental stage, Collet surmises that there may be an element of natural fractal geometry in the creation of the patterns.

This element of surprise, she adds, is typical of working with living materials. 'As designers, we are formally trained to work with "dead and inert" materials that we can control. Few know how to work with living materials; you have to know how to feed them, nurture them and eventually how to kill them or harvest their production. It's always very tricky to try and control the process, especially as I work with very experimental techniques.' She believes that the challenge for mass production of mycelium materials will be in the aesthetics. 'They tend to look a little brown, not terribly exciting. That's one of the challenges I want to take on.'

designandlivingsystems.com

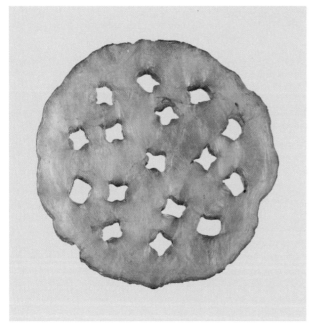

The Growduce device is described as a combination of bio-composter and 3D printer and is designed to transform organic household waste into a cellulose-based mouldable organic polymer.

The material output is influenced by the ingredients. Various properties, such as colour and odour, can be manipulated by different additions.

Growduce

Guillian Graves and Aakriti Jain

Industrial designer Guillian Graves and biologist Aakriti Jain have combined their expertise and experience in Growduce, which promises a sustainable alternative to materials such as plastics.

Graves and Jain have developed a machine that can produce a mouldable organic polymer made of cellulose that could one day allow consumers to 'grow' their own 3D products, opening the tantalizing possibility of a home circular micro-factory in which waste can be endlessly recycled into new products.

'We have imagined a future where small micro-factories will be the go-to machines to create everyday consumer products,' say the designers. Jain envisages that Growduce could eventually be a standard device in every home, 'as easy to use as a coffee machine'.

Described by Graves as a combination of bio-composter and 3D printer, each Growduce contains a symbiotic colony of bacteria and yeast – or scoby – in a ceramic chamber. More often seen in fermented drinks manufacture, a scoby requires very little attention other than maintaining correct temperature and pH. Fed with organic household waste, the micro-organisms produce layers of cellulose that can be harvested, then dried in moulds to create everyday objects. Different additives influence the properties, colour and odour of the cultivated membrane, which could prove surprisingly versatile.

For instance, adding soothing aloe vera to the cellulose could allow it to be used as a homemade 'plaster'.

Growduce is still at the conceptual stage, but the duo envisage future applications that could range from clothing to fuel sticks or batons to heat the home – all produced on site and entirely from waste.

As Graves observes, current recycling procedure often involves transporting waste over long distances, which has an environmental impact of its own. Growduce reflects the way that in nature the waste of each species becomes a resource for other species and produces new material. 'Growduce offers a new way to recycle organic waste locally and transform it into new objects that are both durable and biodegradable,' says Graves, adding that the project also invites us to reconsider our perception of bacteria and micro-organisms from 'harmful' to 'useful'.

guilliangraves.com

The Grow It Yourself
Krown Design

Netherlands-based Krown Design has pioneered a mycelium-based home kit that allows anyone to grow their own creation in just a few days, for just a few euros. The Grow It Yourself (GIY) material arrives in dried form. A combination of stabilized mycelium and agricultural waste, it is reactivated with water and ready to use in four to five days.

The kit is available with a simple cardboard template for a lampshade, but the sky's the limit for those with imagination. The instructions suggest using anything from a cake tin to a sandcastle bucket as a mould, or creating a unique shape using 3D-printed designs or small-scale thermoforming, perhaps at a local maker space. When the finished object has been allowed to grow for a further six days or so, then dried out, it is light, durable and compostable when it reaches the end of its useful life.

For those without the patience to grow their own, Krown offers a range of readymade designs crafted in similar material. Lampshades and a pouf and table are currently available, all grown to order.

The Krown label, part of Ecovative Europe (the name combines 'eco' and 'innovative'), is a collaboration between Designers of the Unusual, founded by Eric Klarenbeek, the packaging and distribution innovators packaging company and biomaterials company Ecovative USA. Its products are created from 'mushroom material', a customizable, sustainable engineered 'wood' made of local raw material bound together with mycelium as a 'living glue'. Natural, safe and versatile,

it is competitive in terms of production cost and offers fire-resistance, buoyancy and insulating properties. Its possibilities are manifold, covering not only products, but also packaging, interiors and architectural applications.

'The material is literally grown, not manufactured,' explain the founders. 'We use a growing organism to transform agricultural waste products like husks from Dutch hemp, flax and corn stalk into a beautiful product that is safe and natural. The plant material produces oxygen during its lifecycle, simultaneously binding CO_2.'

Opening up the potential for creating products with a negative carbon footprint, the production process sequesters CO_2 rather than emitting it. After use, the product can be disposed without harming the environment and breaks down to a fertilizer.

The company applies its environmentally friendly philosophy throughout the production process. Even its 3D-printed moulds are made of renewable biopolymer. They can be shredded and reprinted repeatedly. The founders aim to 'make the production cycle smaller, smarter and local. Striving for a less plastic and oil-dependent economy, now is the time to introduce new possibilities and bring alternatives to the surface.'

krown-design.com

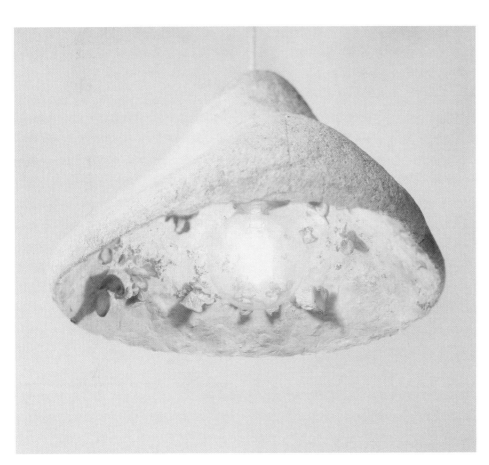

Mycelium products from
lampshades to tables are
sold pre-grown or as
grow-your-own kits.

This page:

A simple mechanism drip-feeds bacteria in order to manipulate the growth of bacterial cellulose in various solutions and pigments to influence the structure, thickness and colour of the material produced.

Opposite:

Gombosova discovered she could produce material akin to strong paper within nine days and material similar to leather within 15 days.

Invisible Resources
Zuzana Gombosova

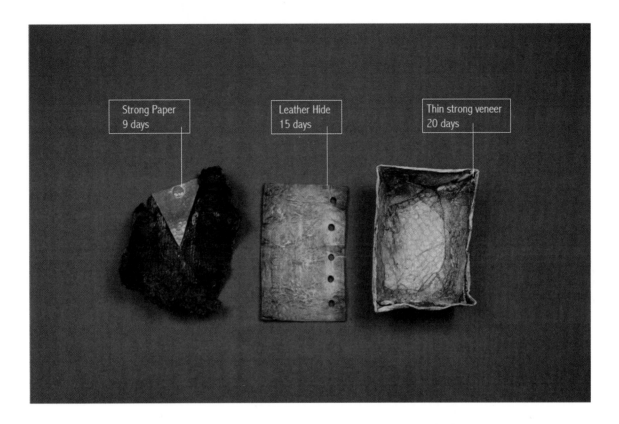

Strong Paper
9 days

Leather Hide
15 days

Thin strong veneer
20 days

In her Invisible Resources project, Slovakian designer Zuzana Gombosova looks to a future where the 'printing' of organic matter is a viable way to produce new materials. 'The future potential of material that can be grown rather than manufactured has been recognized and developed during the last decade by both scientists and designers alike,' says Gombosova. Her work focuses on the biological material bacterial cellulose which, as its name suggests, is a form of cellulose produced by living bacteria. Gombosova has experimented with different patterns of feeding and nurturing the bacteria to control its growth – in effect, she says, 'a biological printer. But instead of printing the material, the device feeds it in the area where we'd like to stimulate the growth.'

The designer initially contacted various leading microbiologists and researched the complex processes by which bacteria and micro-organisms function. She then moved on to growing and cultivating micro-organisms herself, eventually identifying Acetobacter xylinum as the most suitable for her purpose. She developed simple mechanisms to drip-feed the bacteria with carefully selected nutrient solutions and pigments to influence the structure, thickness and colour of the material produced.

Gombosova, whose background is in fashion and textile design, holds a master's degree in Material Futures from Central Saint Martins, London. She has a strong interest in manufacturing processes, critical thinking, research and speculative design. 'How could this alter our current perception and understanding of consumer products?' she asks. 'Would the patience required in using growth processes to acquire goods lead to changes in attitudes towards material culture? Could it lead to new ways of material engineering?'

And, she adds, 'By employing technology in order to manipulate organic matter, I also aim to question our constant efforts to control nature and its unpredictable patterns.'

made-from-malai.com

Botanical Craft

Carole Collet

Botanical Craft revisits the traditional craft of gourd moulding, which has been practised in China for hundreds of years.

The project is part of the Design and Living Systems Lab at Central Saint Martins, London (see page 205), directed by Professor Carole Collet. Some of the most successful examples of gourd moulding were created during China's Qing dynasty in the 18th century. Small, malleable gourds, still on the vine, were enclosed in gracefully shaped moulds with patterns carved on the inside; the mature, ripened gourds took on not only the shape of the mould, but also the intricately carved patterns, and successful examples were regarded as works of art as well as useful containers. The durability and longevity of the final article is proved by the fact that 18th-century moulded gourds still exist today, as museum pieces and collectors' items.

Botanical Craft uses the same technique, but with a more practical goal in mind: the development of a new production chain which grows entire items, rather than material that needs to be processed before being made into a 3D product. It draws on a variety of gourds; these fleshy, hard-skinned fruits grow best in hot, humid conditions, but can also easily be cultivated in continental climates. The moulds are made first as wooden shapes, and then the final shapes are thermoformed. They are applied as the gourd begins to grow, bolted in place, and left until the gourd is fully mature. The shaped gourd is then harvested and left to dry; during the drying process its inner flesh shrivels away and its outer skin hardens until it resembles soft wood. The intended result of Botanical Craft, a work in progress when Radical Matter was published, is a collection of elegant contemporary vessels. This will be a pioneering example of a slow, horticultural production mode – a total contrast to the more usual rapid manufacturing model. Sunlight and water are the only inputs and, of course, being composed of vegetable matter these items are entirely biodegradable.

There have been various challenges along the way. First, as the original Chinese gourd moulders also found, this is an unpredictable process. 'You make a mould, place it on a gourd, but you have no idea how big that gourd will become, even on the same plant,' says Collet. 'One gourd might really fill the mould, but the mould next to it might be only half filled. You need a lot to get any good examples.' Also, some shapes are difficult to achieve. 'I want to see how far I can push the gourd from its natural curved form, but sharp corners are really tricky, and some have collapsed in on themselves during the drying process.' Collet has been experimenting with different finishes and has found that when the material is sanded, it resembles marble. 'I want to create sanded and polished vessels that people don't know were grown on a plant,' she says.

In the future, she envisages people becoming interested in growing their own products, just as they are currently interested in growing their own food. 'I can see people getting into the DIY aspect,' she says. 'People could rent moulds, or 3D print them. The technique could also be deployed in countries such as Africa, where the plants grow really well, to help communities develop new crafts.' And, she adds, while it may be difficult to achieve uniform products, even imperfect examples can still function as containers. 'Whether they are beautifully moulded or not, they still have a function; failed ones still work, they're just not as good-looking!'

designandlivingsystems.com

This page:

A thermoformed mould is bolted onto the
young gourd. As it grows the fruit takes
the shape of the mould.

Opposite:

Once the gourd is fully matured the mould
is removed and the fruit harvested.

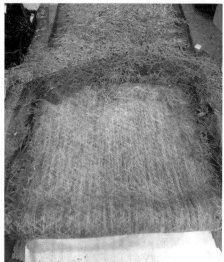

Working primarily with
oat and wheat, Scherer
buries templates into the
soil. These act as moulds,
channelling the root systems.

LIVING MATERIALS

Interwoven
Diana Scherer

German artist Diana Scherer, who lives and works in Amsterdam, uses her work to explore our relationship with the natural environment and the human desire to control nature. Particularly focused on plant processes that happen underground, she describes herself as 'captivated by the root system, with its hidden, underground processes; it is considered the brain of the plant by plant neurobiologists.'

Referring to 'the brain of the plant' is not as far-fetched as it may sound. Scherer cites Charles Darwin's book The Power of Movement in Plants. 'He describes how roots do not passively grow down, but move and observe. A root navigates, knows what's up and down, observes gravity and localizes moisture and chemicals. Darwin discovered that plants are a lot more intelligent than everybody thought. For contemporary botanists, this buried matter is still a wondrous land. There is a global investigation to discover this hidden world. I also want to explore it and apply the "intelligence" of plants in my work.'

Scherer's work includes her Interwoven project and collaborations with biologists and ecologists at Radboud University in Nijmegen, the Netherlands. Working primarily with oat and wheat plants, she buries templates in the soil that act as moulds, channelling the plants' root systems. The resulting geometric structures become beautiful pieces of woven art that resemble textiles or tapestries, and are strong and resilient. Scherer has discovered that, while oat and wheat roots grow quickly and are easy to train, other roots such as daisies grow more slowly and are less easy to form. This discovery could, in the future, influence the rapid pace of mass production, should this project find a commercial application (Scherer is experimenting with pieces such as rugs and exploring the possibility of growing clothing underground). These living materials are currently also ephemeral; each piece lasts only a few weeks before shrivelling away harmlessly, leaving no waste.

Scherer's initial inspiration came from an earlier project, Nurture Studies. The root structure of plants grown in pots was exposed when the pots were broken and Scherer noticed the differences in root-growth patterns and textures for different plants. A graduate in fine art and photography from the Gerrit Rietveld Academie in Amsterdam, as an artist she was reminded of yarn and inspired to take a more structured approach to 'weaving' roots underground. Scherer was named 2016 New Material Fellow by Het Nieuwe Instituut arts institute in Rotterdam; the mentorship was awarded to help her further develop Interwoven and explore its practical applications.

dianascherer.nl

The end results of
Scherer's work are
complex tapestries
of geometric patterns
formed by manipulated
root growth.

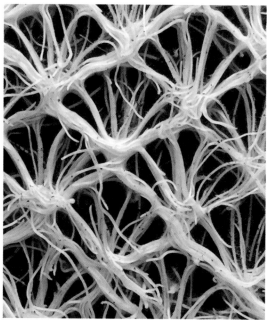

LIVING MATERIALS

Car Fossil, part of the
Cabinet of Anthropogenic
Specimens by Yesenia
Thibault-Picazo.

8
Future Mining

—

Scientists have concluded: humanity has now had such a huge impact on Earth that we have entered a new geological epoch known as the Anthropocene. As a result, we are beginning to witness the discovery and exploration of new raw materials that carry the legacy of industries past. Material resources of the future will be mined from strata of man-made mineral and plastic composites, and fished from shifting oceanic islands of waste. In response, designers have speculated and reimagined the future of geology, encouraging us to redefine our current notions of what is natural or man-made.

In August 2016 at the International Geological Congress in Cape Town the expert delegates argued that the 12,000-year Holocene era of respective climate stability has truly come to an end and should be declared as having officially given way to the new human-centric Anthropocene era.

This epoch, in theory, actually began some time in the mid-20th century; the key marker was in the 1950s when numerous nuclear bomb tests dispersed radioactive elements across the globe. This, compounded with other human-generated industrial-scale pollutants, has served to corrupt the ecological mechanics of the planet and alter the material make-up of the Earth, sea and air.

From the phenomenal amount of concrete and plastic pollution, to soot from industry and even the bones left by the proliferation of the domestic chicken (almost 60 billion are killed each year around the world), humanity has left its mark on the planet.

Geologically speaking, the fruits of the Anthropocene are yet to be witnessed. We are literally at the very start of the era as an epoch will usually span tens of millions of years. However, the acceleration of human industry has already made irreversible and permanent changes to the planet to the point that artificial geological phenomena are being documented worldwide. As a result, designers are beginning to consider not only the complications caused by these vast ecological changes, but also the potential.

Geological material of the future will bear witness to man's dominion over nature and will be human-generated. Materials such as plastiglomerate and 'Plasma rock' will become ubiquitous. The former, a composite of plastic and organic beach sediment, is increasingly found on polluted beaches. This mix of organic and man-made waste could be an abundant resource of the future, to be gathered along the world's coastlines. Plasma rock is a by-product of an emerging technology beginning to be employed to tackle historic landfills. The thermal process converts landfill waste, an indiscriminate blend of organic and man-made material into 'syngas', a synthetic natural gas that can be used for fuel. The residual molten material turns into a lava-like substance, Plasma rock, which is mechanically strong and environmentally stable. This by-product is currently being explored as construction material among other applications.

As the realization of the implications of the Anthropocene begins to hit home, radical ways to tackle the uncertainty of our future are being sought; while far-sighted, extreme innovators are looking beyond the skies for new habitats beyond our planet and considering extra-terrestrial agricultural solutions, others are broaching more immediate interventions closer to home.

Designers are rethinking the potential of pollution: why mine something native and diminishing such as fossil fuels when we could harvest abundant pollutants and draw alien man-made matter from the **Earth**, **Sea** and **Air**?

1

3

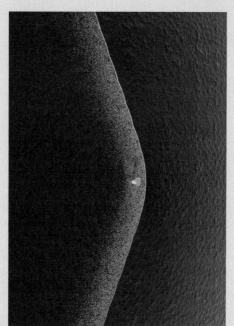

2

4

5

6

9

7

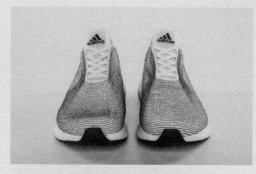

8

Earth

Man-made materials that do not break down are becoming the new raw material for designers and makers. Either reclaimed from the earth as they went in or melded with other materials and organic matter through geological processes.

1 — Plastiglomerate Samples by Kelly Jazvac
2 — Craft in the Anthropocene by Yesenia Thibault-Picazo
3 — New Geology by Jorien Wiltenburg

Sea

Every piece of plastic ever made still exists today. Around 8 million tons of this finds its way into the oceans each year. Creatives and industrial innovators have begun to tackle the issue of plastic pollution. Not only in the search for alternatives, but in the reclaim and reappropriation of existing synthetic material that has already been deposited in our waterways. The recycling of this material not only aids in the battle to save our oceans and marine life, but also deters the production of new virgin materials.

4 — Gyrecraft by Studio Swine
5 — The Ocean Cleanup by Boyan Slat
6 — Ocean Plastic by Parley for the Oceans

Air

Air pollution and smog is a purely anthropogenic creation, a by-product of industry that we have come to accept as a necessary evil and an inherent symptom of our ongoing industrial evolution. Designers and innovators are beginning to question this notion and argue that we can reclaim these invisible pollutants to give the harmful matter new forms and new purpose.

7 — Roet by Martens & Visser
8 — KAALINK and Air-Ink by Graviky Labs
9 — Smog Free Projects by Daan Roosegaarde

Jan Zalasiewicz

Geologist Jan Zalasiewicz, professor of palaeobiology at the University of Leicester, is chair of the Anthropocene Working Group of the International Commission on Stratigraphy.

The term Anthropocene refers to the relatively recent time period when human activities such as mining, agriculture and urbanization have physically altered the Earth's structure and cycles. The evidence for the Anthropocene can be put into three very large buckets: physical, chemical and biological. Until about 1750 such changes were very slow. They accelerated rapidly in the post-war boom of the mid-20th century. In the early 1950s, layers of geological strata round the world were sprinkled with detectable amounts of plutonium and caesium from nuclear tests. This was not the beginning of the Anthropocene, but it's a useful marker. The key thing about the Anthropocene is its trajectory. The former stable background is now changing its character very rapidly – and this has taken place in the space of one human lifetime. Humans are altering the geological make-up of the planet.

A lot of human impacts are negative, or storing up trouble. Some changes, though, aren't necessarily in that category. For instance, we are very good at reshaping chemical compounds into new forms. There are getting on for 5,000 natural minerals. Humans came in and started making what are, in effect, minerals; these number around 187,000 and climbing, a dramatic increase in mineralogical diversity. Some of these new materials might become key in the Anthropocene conditions of the future.

Plastiglomerates are a good example of human and natural processes combining, but they are a microscopic part of the changes taking place. The really big resources of the future are landfill sites, which are enormous by comparison: kilometres across, thousands of metres deep. They contain metals, plastics, human-made and organic material in the most incredible mixtures, mixtures not at all present anywhere in the natural world. Physically, chemically and biologically we are creating something quite alien to the Earth.

You might also wonder what you can do with the subsoil beneath the city. The mashed-up remains of former buildings, mixed up with soil, can form a layer tens of metres thick. There is also the stuff dumped as waste by metal and coal mines: billions of tons of stuff that is a potential resource.

The next 50 years will be critical. We need to decarbonize industry pretty quickly. The effectiveness and cost of renewables such as solar is getting better all the time. I have colleagues working on ways to extract metals without some of the damaging consequences of big holes in the ground. The question is how quickly we will adapt. The technosphere refers to the way that human-built structures and technology are becoming a new system, rather like the biosphere. A whole lot of people are pushing and pulling, but no one is in charge, and it is evolving by natural selection. For example, mobile phones suddenly spread and became a huge influence. No one could have predicted that until mobiles arrived, and we can't predict what will come next.

There's clearly a space for new thinking in design. Our present course is not sustainable. The way we use huge amounts of energy, the way we use materials: one way or another there will have to be modification. Development and sustainability is partly material conception and partly societal. A whole lot of people will have to talk to each other in realistic ways.

There is a bumpy path ahead but some aspects offer hope. We now have a better picture of the unintended consequences of our success over the past centuries. We can use that knowledge to develop new materials that might help. Humans are ingenious creatures – and our practical ingenuity will certainly be needed.

New stones found on Kamilo Beach in Hawaii
have been dubbed plastiglomerates. The alien
stones are composed of a blend of molten
plastic and organic beach sediment including
sand, wood, coral and basalt rock. The
discovery is tangible evidence of the
effect of humanity and industry on natural
ecosystems.

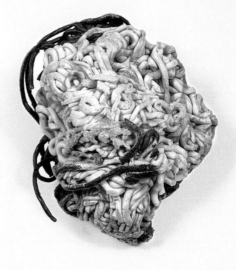

Plastiglomerate Samples

Kelly Jazvac

Since the mid-20th century, approximately six billion tons of plastic has been manufactured. With much of this ending up in landfill or the oceans, this plastic persists, preserved in the ground or bonded to organic material.

In 2006, while surveying the plastic waste washed up on Kamilo Beach, a remote stretch of polluted sand on Hawaii's Big Island, oceanographer Charles Moore discovered an alien plastic material. This discovery turned out to be plastic waste that had fused with organic sediment to create a new type of stone. This hybrid blend of organic and man-made waste consisted of a mix of molten plastic and beach sediment, including sand, wood, coral and basalt rock.

Dubbed 'plastiglomerate', this discovery has the potential to become a fossil of the future, signalling the impact of human pollution and acting as a permanent marker of the Anthropocene in our planet's geological record.

Following the recommendation of Moore, geologist Patricia Corcoran and artist Kelly Jazvac began a study of the 'stone' that was appearing on Kamilo Beach. While the hybrid material was found on the shore of Hawaii, much of the plastic content of the compound was believed not to be native to the island, suggesting that the phenomenon is not a localized one.

Jazvac presents these plastiglomerate samples as artefacts of the Anthropocene, as evidence of the negative and mutating impact of plastic pollution and as a warning sign for what inaction may mean for the future.

kellyjazvac.com

Craft in the Anthropocene
Yesenia Thibault-Picazo

'Craft in the Anthropocene' presents an imagined future, a series of 'novel rocks' that have occurred as a result of human activity, based on real anthropogenic facts and events.

Thibault-Picazo's Cabinet of Anthropogenic Specimens is an assortment of material experiments. Focusing on various man-made materials that are distinctive to our anthropogenic epoch and ubiquitous to our way of life, the designer mimicked geological processes to manipulate the samples. Plastics, aluminium, steel, concrete, glass and textiles were manipulated to become speculative future fossils.

Giving real context to her speculations, the designer envisages the various crafts and industries that future anthropogenic materials may be applied to. She often references specific events or occurrences that have led to the accumulation of a specific material in the ground.

Cumbrian Bone Marble, for example, is an imagined future rock. The stone and bone composite is theoretically derived from the 2001 Foot and Mouth outbreak in the north-west of England. The epidemic led to the slaughter and burial of millions of livestock carcasses, thus depositing an unprecedented amount of animal bone into the ground and giving the Earth a very specific content.

Thibault-Picazo depicts a future in which natural resources are not depleted as such but are instead replaced by new alternative 'neo-natural' minerals. These wealthy deposits of waste matter may be harvested and utilized in future crafts and industries.

cargocollective.com/yeseniatp

This page:

The Cabinet of Anthropogenic Specimens by Thibault-Picazo is a collection of speculative future fossils derived from years of human activity. The samples are created by applying simulated, slow geological processes to human generated materials. These include plastics, aluminium, steel, concrete, glass, textile and bone from livestock.

Opposite:

Chiselled human fossil for the Karlsruhe's Cabinet of Future Geology is part of the Anthropogenic Specimens. The speculative fossil is a composed of city centre sediment and suggests that increasing urbanization will change the mineral content of stone and rock found in the urban geology.

In Craft in the Anthropocene,
Thibault-Picazo further
speculates about the
positioning of future
material resources in craft
practices. The designer
created vessels and tools out
of the speculative materials
to give additional context to
her futuristic visions.

The Thames Aluminium Vessel
is composed of metal sediment
harvested from the bed of
the River Thames. In a
scenario in the future the
resource is derived after
years of industrial aluminium
production has caused an
accumulation of metal residue
in the UK's riverbeds.
The designer proposes that
this pollution should be
a potential material resource
in the future.

The designer presents
reclaimed plastic as
a sought-after material
of the future. The PPC
(Pacific Plastic Crust)
mortar is composed of
material harvested from the
prominent plastic pollution
deposits in the Pacific Ocean.

Cumbrian Bone Marble, part of Craft in the Anthropocene, is an imagined future rock derived from a specific event in history, the 2001 Foot and Mouth epidemic. The disease outbreak resulted in the slaughter and burial of millions of cows and sheep across the UK. Cumbria was the worst affected area. The speculative future rock is mined from wealthy deposits of animal bone in the ground.

Cross-Section Geology, part of New Geology
by Jorien Wiltenburg, is a series of
speculative rocks composed of strata
of waste material. Each piece is made up
of trash from a specific location, bearing
the material legacy of human activity in
these environments.

New Geology

Jorien Wiltenburg

Inspired by the discoveries of various artificial geological phenomena around the globe, Jorien Wiltenburg set out to challenge our understanding of nature.

Referencing the glass beach in California, an artificial piece of coastline made up of washed-up trash, and the discovery of 'synthetic' stones or plastiglomerate in natural ecology, Wiltenburg believes that these phenomena are proof of the permanent altering of the Earth's geology. Wiltenburg suggests that nature itself should be redefined to represent the contemporary make up of the planet we now inhabit.

In the ongoing New Geology project, the designer attempts to anticipate the minerals and geological strata of our future by applying various processes and treatments to amassed waste material. The result is a library of geo-mimetic artefacts that are composed of anthropogenic matter.

In the Future Stones series, Wiltenburg attempted to simulate accelerated geological transformations. Compounds of foam, aluminium, plastic, textiles and glass were subjected to heat and pressure, creating curious futuristic visions of geology.

Cross-Section Geology took the designers' geo-mimicry to a whole new level in which the provenance of the waste material became key to the output. The designer created speculative site-specific strata of futuristic fossilized matter. From the beach to the dump, the content of the artefacts tell the story of the lives lived on those sites.

The designer believes that by understanding a new definition of nature we can build a positive future relationship with the Earth.

'When we embrace this new Anthropocene nature we can create something positive out of it. That's why I wanted to get people to question their notion of what nature is,' Wiltenburg explains.

jorienwiltenburg.nl

Cut Trough is a collection of waste-based tiles resembling futuristic marble. Wiltenburg combines polyester resin with plastic bags, textiles and industrial packing straps to create conglomerate hard materials that are then laser-cut and polished.

FUTURE MINING

Gyrecraft
Studio Swine

Ocean gyres are circular currents in the ocean basin where plastic and other debris is swept up and concentrated. There are five major oceanic gyres: the North Atlantic, the South Atlantic, the North Pacific, the South Pacific and the Indian Ocean. Each is home to different native wildlife and different industries, and yet all share the common plight of plastic pollution.

Design provocateurs Alexander Groves and Azusa Murakami of Studio Swine travelled 1,000 nautical miles from the Azores to the Canaries through the North Atlantic gyre collecting plastic debris along the way. As the plastic pieces are forced through spiralling patterns in the current they are broken down into smaller and smaller fragments. These fragments become separated and spread across huge expanses of ocean, utterly ubiquitous and yet laborious to recover.

The designers' expedition resulted in the Gyrecraft project. Studio Swine define the term as 'The maritime activity of transforming plastic pollution found at sea into new objects'. The result of the project is a collection of artefacts, each dedicated to one of the world's major gyres. Within each design the team would consider not only the material content of the piece, but also the craft that could appropriately be employed in the vicinity of each gyre. The result is that each piece has a unique identity reflecting its geography.

The North Atlantic gyre article, for example, pays homage to the decorative craft of scrimshaw. This was a traditional technique employed by those involved in the now-obsolete whaling industry of the region.

With their on-board solar extruder, the team processed the collected plastic waste and reinvented it into new objects. Designed in collaboration with Andrew Friend, the solar extruder is a simplified iteration of industrial plastic processing machinery. The manually operated, portable device is powered by sunlight. It works by melting the plastic and piping it in layers to create new solid forms that can then be shaped and crafted by hand.

In Gyrecraft, Studio Swine not only highlights the plight of the oceans and the proliferation of micro plastic in the world's waterways, but the designers also elevate the material by juxtaposing it with craft and tradition. Investing time and skill into it, consequently, they turn a polluting threat into a desirable resource.

studioswine.com

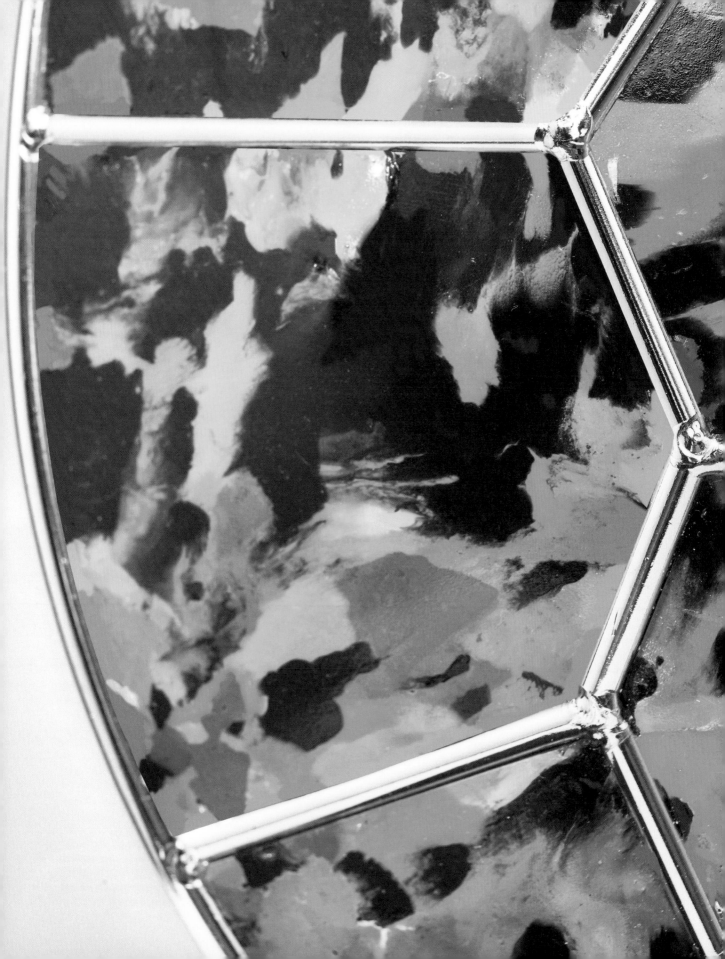

Gyrecraft is defined by Studio Swine as
'the maritime activity of transforming
plastic pollution found at sea into new
objects'. The studio created five artefacts;
each represents one of the five ocean gyres.

The Indian Ocean gyre object, composed of
sea plastic, mother-of-pearl, aluminium,
steel, brass and rope, is a tribute to
the Sentinelese people of the Andaman
Islands. As the last pre-Neolithic tribe
in the world, they are isolated from modern
industry, yet they are still affected by
plastic pollution.

Studio Swine pay homage to the culture and distinctive crafts of the remote island communities of the South Pacific through the creation of the South Pacific Gyre object. Harvested ocean plastic is blended to create a surface reminiscent of tortoiseshell and is combined with rich materials such as hard wood, gold-plated steel and brass.

The North Atlantic gyrecraft object references the past-time crafts employed in the now-obsolete whaling industry of the Azores. Scrimshaw involved the hand carving of intricate designs into whale teeth.
Studio Swine combined hand-moulded sea plastic with reclaimed mahogany, rope and brass to create a contemporary iteration of a scrimshaw artefact.

The Ocean Cleanup
Boyan Slat

The Ocean Cleanup, founded by Dutch inventor Boyan Slat, develops technologies to extract, prevent and intercept plastic pollution. The project's goal is to initiate the largest ocean clean-up in history.

The Ocean Cleanup is an energy-neutral design powered by natural ocean currents and acts as an artificial coastline to concentrate debris while causing no harm to sea life. The plastic flotsam, once gathered and concentrated, is easier to extract for recycling.

The array is designed to be modular, durable, to be able to withstand unruly conditions and to be scalable for implementation in various different oceanic environments. For instance, small-scale systems can be made in order to intercept plastic waste near land. Or multi-kilometre installations can be deployed to clean up the five gyre garbage patches of the oceans. The organization's aim for the Ocean Cleanup array is to install the system in the Great Pacific Garbage Patch in 2020. The team projects that the technology could harvest almost half of the area's debris within 10 years, collecting an estimated 70,000,000 kg (154,300,000 lbs) of potential reusable waste.

The Ocean Cleanup plans to set up ocean plastic-processing centres, where the plastic could potentially be used to make oil. This process has a net positive carbon impact and consumes less energy than extracting fossil crude oil. Alternatively, the harvest could be used in the production of 100% recycled plastic products.

While the successful implementation of the Ocean Cleanup could help in striving towards a clean future for the oceans, believing that they can only partially fix the problem, the team continues to campaign for greater awareness of plastic consumption. From the individual to governments and corporations, it is the responsibility of everyone to end our addiction to plastic.

theoceancleanup.com

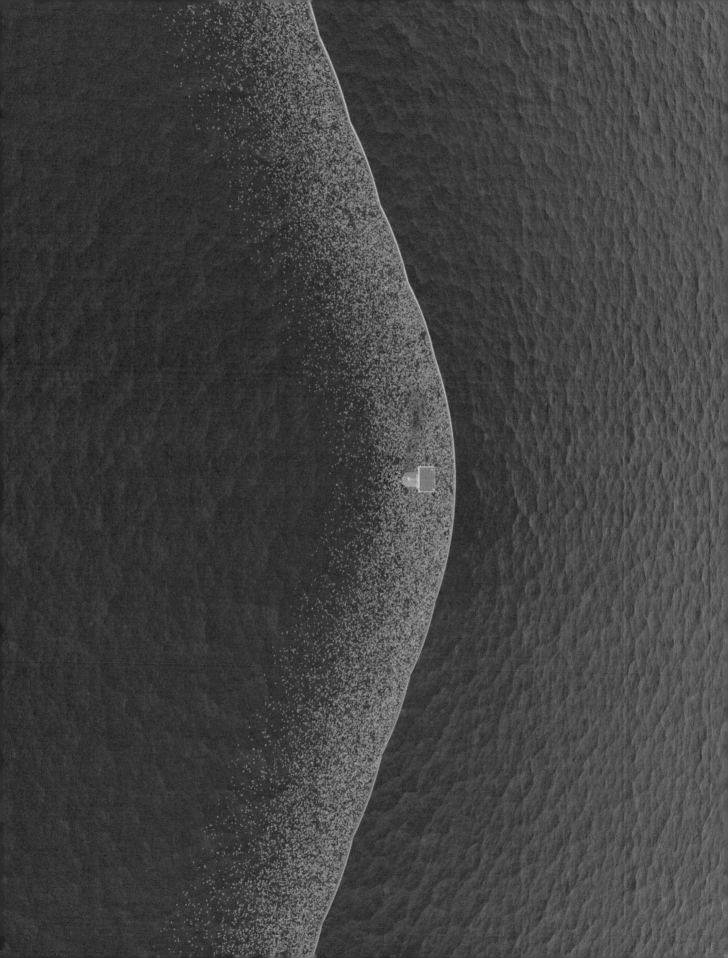

Ocean Plastic

Parley for the Oceans

Approximately 5.25 trillion pieces of plastic are currently breaking down in the oceans at any one time. Once the plastic has degraded to a micro scale it is consumed by fish and sea life. As well as endangering the ocean's wildlife itself, the micro plastic often inadvertently finds its way into the human food stream and into our own bodies.

Founded by Cyrill Gutsch, Parley for the Oceans is dedicated to the conservation of the world's oceans. The organization rallies creatives from all over the world, bringing together artists, designers, inventors and scientists as well as well-known global brands. All have the common goal of finding creative solutions to the world's oceanic concerns.

Committed not only to preventing more plastic from entering the waterways, Parley and its collaborators have conceived initiatives to reclaim existing plastic pollution and find purpose for the waste.

As a long-term partner of the organization, Adidas is guided by the Parley A.I.R. strategy. A simple three-tiered methodology; first, avoid virgin plastic wherever possible, second, intercept plastic waste and third, redesign the plastic economy.

Through a series of product innovations and developments, Adidas has had several successful product launches containing Parley Ocean Plastic®, from high-performance sportswear, such as the Real Madrid football jersey in yarns of recycled Ocean Plastic to the Ultra Boost Uncaged trainer.

Without compromising on the technical performance of the shoe, Adidas were able to cut out nearly all virgin material from its composition. The lace, heel, webbing, heel lining and sock liner cover are made of 100% recycled PET, while the upper is 95% Parley Ocean Plastic®, all of which was collected from the Maldives. The upper alone of each shoe reuses 11 plastic bottles.

Parley Ocean Plastic® is more than a material. It is a technology that has defined a whole new resource, one which could not only sustain an industrial need, but could also simultaneously save our oceans.

parley.tv — adidas.co.uk/parley

Left:

The crew of the Sea Shepherd ship, the Sam Simon, removed 72 km of illegal gillnets from the waters of the Southern Ocean. The strategic recovery took over three weeks to complete during their record-breaking Operation Icefish campaign. Parley for the Oceans gives new life to the netting retrieved by Sea Shepherd.

Below:

Parley partners, Sustainable Coastlines Hawaii, use a sand sifter to separate micro plastics from the beach during a collaborative clean-up in Hawaii. The Adidas x Parley shoe (opposite) is composed of illegal gillnets and Parley Ocean Plastic®. The upper alone of each shoe gives new life to 11 plastic bottles.

This page:

Roet by Martens & Visser is
an investigation into the
potential of soot as a design
material. The design duo
initially created a pigment
by capturing soot inside an
oil lamp.

Opposite:

The designers experimented
with using soot pigment as a
fabric dye to create textural
surface patterns. The pair
wanted to highlight the
extremely polluting nature
of the textile industry by
literally using pollution in
the design process.

Roet
Martens & Visser

Black soot is one of the biggest causes of the hothouse effect. A by-product of numerous industrial processes, the pollutant is believed to contain carcinogenic material. It has been blamed for the deteriorating health of the inhabitants of many of the world's urban metropolises and industrial centres.

Turning pollution into a design medium, Jetske Visser and Michiel Martens developed a technique that uses harvested soot to dye textiles. The resulting colour and intensity of the pigmentation is greatly dependent on the duration the soot is collected for. In this project the pair wanted to highlight the fact that the textile industry is one of the most polluting of all industries by literally using the pollution in the design of the fabrics.

The designers were invited to run a workshop based on the Roet project during Beijing Design Week 2013. Working with students from the Central Academy of Fine Arts Beijing, the team collected soot and ash from a range of sources in the polluted city. These included temples where incense is burned, street BBQ's, which are prolific in the city, and coal stoves used for heating homes, all of which contribute to the city's pollution problem.

Using the amassed soot and ash, Martens and Visser created pigment for wax crayons, screen-printing ink and lacquer capable of colouring materials such as wood, textiles and paper. Visser continues to collect soot from big cities around the world, building a collection of site-specific pigments.

martens-visser.com

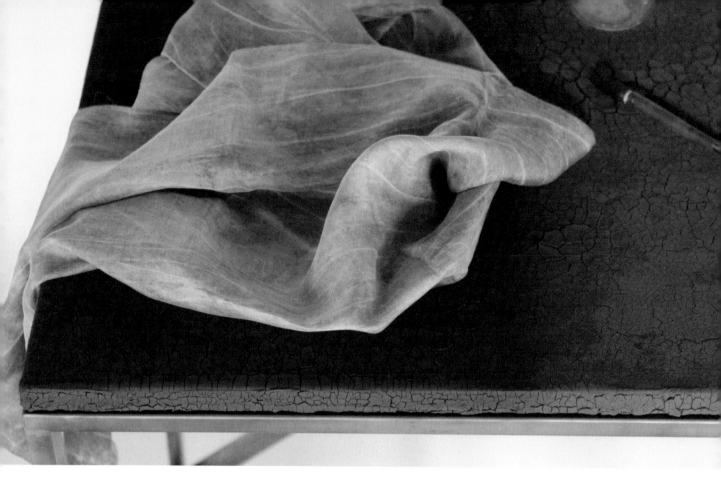

Martens & Visser ran a workshop in Beijing
based on their Roet project. During the
workshop they collected polluting soot and
ash from numerous sources within the city.
The team then developed multiple pigments
for various media, including screen-printing
inks, crayons and lacquers.

FUTURE MINING

Post tailpipe Particulate Matter Samples|

Taxi- 3 years- 1364 cc

Truck- 4 years- Cummins ISB 9

Etios Taxi- 4 years- 13

5 years- 350cc

Tiger

15MM MARKER
APPROX 130 MINS
OF DIESEL CAR
POLLUTION

AIR-I

收集空氣污染的墨條。淨化成筆中墨灣墨水。由亞洲街道開發。心跳難您后戲。
Every drop of ink in this pen has been created from air pollution. Proudly made by Tiger
The beer of Asia's streets. This product is under development/testing. Please use at your
own discretion. Recommended usage - ages 8 and above. Innovated by GRAVIKY LABS
Disclaimer - graviky.com/air-ink

Graviky Labs collaborated
with Tiger Beer to trial
the KAALINK technology in
Hong Kong and Bangalore.
The collaboration produced
150 litres of Air-Ink, which
is equivalent to 2,500 hours
of vehicle emissions. The
Air-Ink was used to create
various media including
marker pens, and was given
to local artists to create
street art.

KAALINK and Air-Ink

Graviky Labs

Air pollution is the modern scourge of many of the world's major cities. Caused by industry and the ineffective filtering of vehicle emissions, the toxicity levels in many metropolises are becoming dangerous. Soot is produced by the incomplete combustion of fossil fuels and is chiefly composed of carbon. What makes these soot particles particularly dangerous is their size. Smaller than dust or mould particles, at 2.5 micro metres or less, the particles find their way into the respiratory system and cause real damage to the human body.

According to Asian Scientist magazine, scientists predict that the death toll from air pollution will reach 6.6 million by 2050 if action is not taken to reduce emissions. Determined to combat this invisible assassin, a pollution-capturing system was conceptualized by Anirudh Sharma at the MIT Media Lab. This spurred the founding of the research group Graviky Labs where the team developed the invention into KAALINK. The device can be retrofitted to many automotive vehicles in order to capture around 95% of Particulate Matter pollution expelled by the engine. This prevents it from ever entering the atmosphere. The system is being piloted and tested to capture pollution particles from both automotive and static sources of air pollution.

The team conceived an innovative application for the captured pollution. They have developed a technique to detoxify the captured particulate matter and transform the molecules into high-quality liquid ink. Able to produce inks in various forms, Air-Ink can be used in screen printing, marker pens and acrylic paint.

A collaboration with Tiger Beer in 2016 saw the prototype system trialled in Hong Kong and Bangalore. The trial produced 150 litres of Air-Ink, equating to roughly 2,500 hours of car emissions. The scaling of such a system could work to heal the atmosphere and reduce the use of more virgin material.

graviky.com

Smog Free Projects
Daan Roosegaarde

Concerned with the blight of toxic air population in urban environments, Dutch designer Daan Roosegaarde and a team of experts have created 'the world largest smog vacuum cleaner'.

The tower runs on green wind energy and minimal amounts of electricity. It uses patented ozone-free ion technology and is capable of cleaning 30,000m³ of air per hour. The portable tower sucks in surrounding air and captures and contains smog particles to emit only clean air. The continuously active tower creates a clean air bubble in a radius around the installation.

Following an initial residency of the tower in Rotterdam, 2016 saw Studio Roosegaarde initiate a Smog Free Tower tour of China. At its first destination, Beijing, the tower processed a volume of 30 million m³ of polluted air over a period of 41 days. China's ministry of Environmental Protection reported 55% cleaner air in the vicinity of the installation.

Believing that in the future waste simply should not exist, Roosegaarde decided to find an application for the smog particles they had collected. Inspired by the fact that the smog is roughly around 42% carbon, which under extreme high pressure turns into diamonds, the team developed the smog-free ring. Each cube-shaped ring encapsulates a condensed cube of smog pulled from 1,000m³ of air.

The Smog Free Tower could aid in the pursuit of a more cyclical future, whereby the air itself can be 'mined' for useful matter, simultaneously purifying the air we breathe of toxic pollutants.

studioroosegaarde.net

Left and below:

Roosegaarde developed the Smog Free Ring, and transforms accumulated pollution into something precious. Each ring represents 1,000m³ of cleaned air.

Opposite:

The Smog Free Tower, by Daan Roosegaarde, runs on clean wind energy and minimal electricity, and is capable of cleaning 30,000m³ of polluted city air per hour.

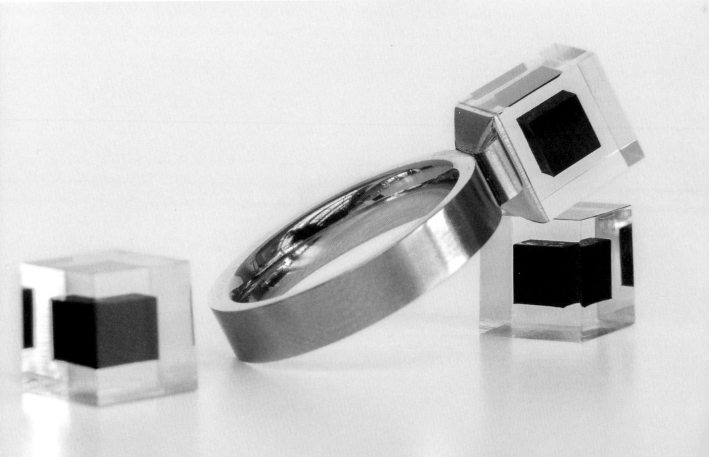

Image Credits

Introduction

Today's Waste, Tomorrow's Raw Material

Natural Assets

Shit, Hair, Dust

Material Connections

Co-Creation

Index

First published in 2018 in the
United States of America by
Thames & Hudson Inc.,
500 Fifth Avenue, New York,
New York 10110

www.thamesandhudsonusa.com

Library of Congress Control Number
2017945555

ISBN 978-0-500-51962-2

Printed in China for
RR Donnelley

About the Authors

Kate Franklin and Caroline Till founded research & design consultancy FranklinTill Studio in 2010. Specializing in design, colour and material research, FranklinTill Studio work with global brands to understand how design and material innovation can impact positive change. Bringing research to life is at the core of their output, curating and producing award-winning publications, exhibitions and events. Editors of globally renowned magazines Viewpoint and Viewpoint Colour, Kate and Caroline regularly contribute to international design conferences, festivals and events.

With a career spanning trend forecasting, design brand strategy, Kate has headed trend and insight departments for design consultancies, trends agencies and global brands and was creative director of The Future Laboratory, before she co-founded FranklinTill Studio

With a background in design and material research, prior to setting up FranklinTill Caroline led projects commissioned by institutions such as the Home Office's Design & Technology Alliance and the Institute of Materials and Mining, facilitating relationships across science, design and technology. Previously responsible for pioneering and directing the Material Futures course at Central Saint Martins, London, Caroline teaches at a number of worldwide academic institutions on the subject of sustainable design practices, design innovation and future materials.

Acknowledgments

Thank you to all the designers, scientists and material innovators who contributed their time and work to be featured in this book.

A special thank you to the experts who gave their time to be interviewed: Carole Collet, Anders Lendager, Julia Lohmann, Zoe Laughlin, Daniel Charney, Joni Steiner, Kate Goldsworthy, Maurizio Montalti & Jan Zalasiewicz.

And finally a huge thank you to the amazing team at FranklinTill Studio:

LEAD RESEARCHER & WRITER
Amy Radcliffe

WRITERS
Hester Lacey
Rob Uhlig

RESEARCHER
Titia Dane

ART DIRECTOR
Laura Gordon